D1131300

CLAY IS THE WORD

ALAN WARNER

Clay is the Word

PATRICK KAVANAGH 1904-1967

THE DOLMEN PRESS

Set in Times Roman type and printed
and published in the Republic of Ireland
by The Dolmen Press Limited
North Richmond Industrial Estate, North Richmond Street, Dublin 1

Distributed outside Ireland, except in the United States of America
and in Canada, by Oxford University Press.
Distributed in the United States of America and in Canada
by Humanities Press Inc.,
450 Park Avenue South, New York, NY 10016

First published 1973

SBN 85105 210 X *bound*
SBN 85105 206 1 *paperback*

CONTENTS

ACKNOWLEDGEMENTS

I am grateful to MacGibbon & Kee Ltd. and to Martin Brian & O'Keeffe Ltd. for permission to quote from copyright material. Peter Kavanagh kindly allowed me to use 'The Gift' and passages from 'Lough Derg', both from *November Haggard*. Austin Clarke and R. S. Thomas generously gave me permission to quote from their poems and I am indebted to W. H. Auden and to Faber & Faber Ltd. for a quotation from *Collected Shorter Poems*.

I would also like to acknowledge the help and courtesy I received from the National Library of Ireland, Dublin University Library and the Library of University College, Dublin. *The Irish Farmers' Journal* and *The Dundalk Democrat* kindly put their files at my disposal. The officials of Telefís Eireann and Radio Eireann were most helpful, especially Colin O'Griofa who unearthed several old radio talks.

Some passages in this book have already appeared in magazine articles. I am grateful to the editors of *A Review of English Literature*, *The Dublin Magazine* and *English* for permission to reprint.

PREFACE

I had never heard or seen the name of Patrick Kavanagh until in 1960 I received a book of poems by post from the Poetry Book Society with the curious title, *Come Dance with Kitty Stobling.* I read the poems and found myself immediately attracted to some of them, though there were others that I didn't fully understand. I knew little of Dublin and I was living in Africa at the time. A little later I came across a reference to Kavanagh and a few lines from *The Great Hunger,* and I knew then that Kavanagh was a poet whose work I must read.

By this time I had moved to Ireland and I was in a better position to follow up my interest in his writing. Indeed I was fortunate enough to meet the poet himself at his home in Inniskeen and also in Dublin. For a time we were on friendly terms, but after my first article on his work, parts of which he disliked, our relationship became more distant, much to my regret.

In writing this book about him I have been keenly aware of his deep distrust of academics. He feared what might happen after his death.

> Apart altogether from eternal damnation, the dangers of death for a writer are terrible with all those American specialists hanging around. There are a few such here in Ireland, too, and poor me is anything but safe if old serjeant Death should recruit me.[1]

Not long after he wrote these words 'old serjeant Death' did indeed recruit him. His published work lies open to the critic and commentator. As Auden said of Yeats:

> Now he is scattered among a hundred cities
> And wholly given over to unfamiliar affections.[2]

In making this first study of an important Irish poet, I trust that I am not approaching him as an academic vulture. My main purpose is to bring his work to the notice of a wider reading public and to reveal something of the background that may make it more intelligible to readers outside Ireland. Kavanagh was a familiar figure in Dublin, and his work was read and much discussed by a number of readers in Ireland. But outside Ireland, and small literary groups in England and America, his work is little known. He opens his wry preface to the *Collected Poems* by remarking: 'I have never been much considered by the English critics.'

Yet Kavanagh was aware that all good writing is universal, not local in its appeal, even though it is tied to a particular place. He was anti-regional and anti-Irish, and he did not wish to be labelled as the peasant poet of the little fields of Monaghan. He remarked, in *The Bell*:

> If anything I had written had the slightest value it would be as true for a Chinese as it would for a man from Drumnaquilla. It would be in fact truer for the man from China, for the man from China would not have his judgment confused by local colour.[3]

I believe that the circle of Kavanagh's readers will widen as the ephemeral and controversial aspects of his work and personality fall away, and the permanent and universal truth of his best poetry remains.

For many years Kavanagh eked out a precarious living by journalism. Much of what he wrote is buried in the files of daily and weekly newspapers. In spite of the publication of his *Collected Pruse* and his brother's selection of articles in *November Haggard*, some of his prose writing is inaccessible. For this reason I have quoted extensively from the *Irish Farmers' Journal* and other sources. I have assumed throughout that Kavanagh's own words provide the most effective guide to his background and his ways of thinking and feeling.

Clay is the word and clay is the flesh
Where the potato-gatherers like mechanised scarecrows move
Along the side-fall of the hill —

The Great Hunger

1

A MAN FROM MONAGHAN

26-9-1917

Dear Teacher,
The cause of my absence from school yesterday was because
we were drawing home the corn and I was sorry I could not
attend my lessons.

Your fond pupil
Patrick Kavanagh.

This early letter, which Kavanagh found in a school copybook
and quoted in an article for the *Irish Farmers' Journal*,[1] opens a
window into his boyhood and the world he belonged to.

He was born on 21 October 1904, in the parish of Inniskeen in
South Monaghan, the fourth child of a large family. James Kavanagh, his father, was a shoemaker, an intelligent and hard-working
man who managed to save money and buy some land. He had a
local reputation for being a good man to 'state' a letter, as good as
a solicitor, and his services were frequently called upon. James
Kavanagh was also a 'bit of a quack'. He went in for home-doctor-
ing and the use of 'infusions', and he was specially noted for his
cure of jaundice. He drew up wills for his neighbours, but after one
of his wills was contested he gave up the practice, in spite of the
fact that the contested will was upheld when the case came before
Judge Johnston, father of Denis Johnston. He wrote love-letters,
too, and his son recalled one that was notable for its brevity.

> One I heard of was to a female near Castleblaney. In the
> current fashion he spurned the word "dear" in front of the
> person's name. In this case he just wrote: "Mary, Pat would
> like to marry you. Will you take him?" Almost equal to
> "Barkis is willing". No bating about the bush.[2]

Patrick Kavanagh gave a brief but illuminating account of his
parents in *The Green Fool*.

> My father was a shoemaker in the good days when a pair of
> shop boots were an insult to any decent man's feet. He was a

11

small lively intelligent man and had among the people a reputation for learning almost as great as the schoolmaster. He played the melodeon till he was forty. He then got married. His passion for music was strong and even after his marriage he found crevices in among his cares in which to play. He was fond of reading but — peace to his soul — he never really got beyond the stage of *Tit Bits* and *Answers*. . . .

My mother was a simple peasant woman, twenty years younger than father. She was without any schooling, but was very shrewd, a good judge of men and animals, and the best measurer of unknown quantities I have ever known.[3]

James Kavanagh supplemented his income as a cobbler by keeping poultry and he studied *Everybody's Guide to Poultry-Keeping* (ca. 1897, price 6d). His son Patrick, turning over the pages of this book long after his father was dead, remarked:

What a lot one can learn from a sixpenny book printed nearly seventy years ago! A winter laying hen could lift a man out of the gutter.

"Do you see," said my father to a neighbour, "a hen on the roof of that loft?" He was pointing to a new loft that he had built.

The neighbour looked hard but could see no hen.

"Well," said my father, "it was the hens that built that loft."

And as was his wont he left the neighbour to ponder on the problem.[4]

When Patrick was born his family had only about half an acre of land around their house — the front garden and the back garden. He remembers vividly their becoming land owners and acquiring a cow.

When I was about four or five a field which ran up to our gardens came for sale. After fierce bidding up to £180 we became landowners.

Shortly afterwards a cow was bought. I remember her well, a strawberry springer purchased from Johnnie White for about £12. Her calf didn't survive and she herself only just managed it. It was in the pre-scientific age and her byre was adorned

12

with all sorts of charms, one of which was a red ribbon tied to her tail.[5]

Monaghan is one of the humblest of the twenty-six counties of the Irish Republic. It has neither mountains nor sea coast. It is separated by Louth from the sea, and it is squeezed against the borders of Ulster between Fermanagh and Armagh. It has been called the county of the little hills. Passing through it one notices the little hills, characteristically divided into triangular fields, because this proved the most suitable way of dealing with drainage. The land is not rich and it is mainly farmed by small farmers. The towns — Monaghan, Castleblayney, Carrickmacross — are small market towns. But although the landscape of Monaghan is unremarkable, it possesses ample pastoral peace and beauty for those who look with the eyes of affection and familiarity. The hills may be small but there are fine views from them away to the sea in the east and the mountains in the north-west. Many a time Kavanagh lifted his eyes from his little fields below the Forth on Rocksavage hill to see the hills of Armagh, or Slieve Gullion, or the sea shining in the distance beyond the plain of Louth.

The world in which Kavanagh grew up was a world in which country superstitions and country traditions still played a large part. He once described it as 'an attractive landscape of small farms and a culture that hadn't changed in a thousand years'.[6] The horse had not yet been superseded by the tractor. There were no radio or television sets in the cottages, and gossip still provided the main entertainment for the people. They would lean over their gates in the evening, or talk at their casual daily meetings by the well or in the shop. 'When my own mother leaned over the gate (though it was only out onto a lane) in days gone by she wouldn't be long without someone to talk to.'[7]

The talk was mainly about people and their doings, about land, jobs, money, marriages, illnesses, deaths. There was little reference to politics or international affairs. 'These rural women could be said to have "nothing to say". Yet they kept on saying it and enjoying each other's company.'[8]

Most trading and commercial activities involved a good deal of talking and provided a little drama to enliven the monotony of country life. The dealer in fowl was known locally as the 'cleaver'.

13

Kavanagh records how it often fell to his lot to catch sick hens to palm off on the cleaver.

> The cleaver's cart could be heard in the distance for there were bells on the pony's harness and the woman of the house had time to be prepared. As soon as the cart stopped at the gate she appeared in the doorway and the cleaver shouted —
> "Have ye any?"
> "I have a few fat ones here that didn't lay an egg this three months — if this fella here could catch them."
> They were all too easy to catch, crippled by age and sickness, but "this fella here", a loose-limbed youth of twelve, had to return with his captives as if he was out of breath.
> The cleaver turned the fowl over and said:
> "It's the last Sacraments them should be getting, Ma'am."
> "That'll do you now, Joe."
> "On account of me often having dales with you, sixpence apiece. I'll get rid of them for you."
> "Oh they may let you out, Joe. I say they may let you out." [9]

Habits of life were conservative in Monaghan and kept to a well-worn pattern. Kavanagh recalls how a local man called Jemmy, who had been away for twenty years in the United States, astonished everybody by his unconventional reply when offered a cup of tea at a kitchen dance or 'stir'.

> Every bockaun would know that you replied, even when you were dying for a 'shrub' (local pronunciation), "No, no, no. Not at all Mrs. Lennon, don't put yourself to the trouble." Instead of that Jemmy just said, "Yes, I'd love a cup." [10]

Later he astonished the company by saying, 'More tea, Mrs. Lennon'.

'Stirs' provided one of the ways in which local people found their entertainment. They have now largely died out and dancing in rural Ireland today takes place in dance halls.

Another traditional social gathering that was still held in Kavanagh's youth was the old-fashioned wake, which he said had been killed by respectability and the rise in the price of whiskey. He remembered being taken to wakes as a boy.

14

One of the earliest wakes I went to was the wake of a very old woman, a neighbour. Myself and a son of the house getting tired during the night went out to the haggard and got ourselves under a blanket of hay in a cut that was made in the rick. We were falling asleep when a bullock got on top of our blanket.[11]

Weddings seemed to be less common than wakes in Kavanagh's youth but old traditions of celebration still survived. In speaking of William Carleton, the nineteenth century Irish novelist, author of *Traits and Stories of the Irish Peasantry* (1832), he remarks that his father, and many others he knew, attended weddings that closely resembled the one described in Carleton's story of 'Shane Fadh's Wedding', including the curious old custom of running for the bottle.

I know my father ran for the bottle, but I never rightly knew how this old ceremony was arranged. As far as I can make out the bottle was in the bride's place and the weddeners, returning after "the knot was tied", started to run from a given start.[12]

Superstition still had a secure footing in the minds of the country people of Monaghan, especially the older ones. Some of them would sooner call in a local wise woman than a doctor. Many popular country cures were still practised. Kavanagh recalled some of these in an article he wrote for the *Irish Farmers' Journal* entitled 'Queer Cures of Yesteryears'.

The cure of mumps was to put an ass's winkers on the child's head and lead it in and out of a pig's sty three times saying each time (in Irish it came down to us)
"Togad do leicana, mucna, mucna." (Take the mumps, pigs, pigs.)
For a stye on the eye a person of the opposite sex pointed a gooseberry thorn nine times at the offending stye.
Any person named McElroy (this may have something to do with the King's servant) was supposed to have the cure of the rose or the erysipilis. A man of that name who lived on our lane had a big practice and many an evening sufferers called at our house to enquire the way. Harry had two cures, a long one and a short one; if you had money it took nine consecutive

15

days with the drink full on to do the trick, but poor, one rub. He merely touched the spot with his hand.[13]

People read supernatural significance into many small occurrences. For instance, it was believed that if a cock crowed before midnight it foretold the death of a relative.

> Many's the time I heard people listening as an old rooster started crowing before midnight. Every face went pale, including my own six-year-old mug, and we all waited in terror till the old woman of the house gave her verdict.
> "Well, what do you think, Mary?"
> "It's not too bad, it's only for a friend (local name for relative) not one of the house."
> "That atself."
> "Once he crowed more nor three times it's only for a friend," Mary explained.
> We all looked up to her with thankfulness. And then we began to speculate as to who ablonging to us was booked for the down train. . . .
> It wasn't eggs, hens and the like were a bother to that cock. He was involved in higher mathematics.[14]

Patrick Kavanagh's younger brother, Peter, compiled a *Dictionary of Irish Mythology* which included many popular superstitions. It was considered unlucky, for example, to walk across a plough; and a plough should always be left facing north. It was said that if a farmer killed a swallow his cows would give blood instead of milk. If a young man wanted a woman to fall in love with him, he should wipe his face in her apron. Patrick, discussing his brother's dictionary remarked:

> Most of these beliefs were strongly held in my day. Indeed I remember clearly seeing (if it wasn't an optical illusion) the crowds of butterflies on the window at night and rightly worried about who was going to die. Butterflies are angels in disguise and coming for the soul of the dead person.[15]

It was not only popular superstitions that flourished. The imagination of the country people was still nourished by stories from Irish mythology, and many local place names were linked

16

with the heroes of the past. It was even said of a huge stone that lay outside the Kavanaghs' door that it had been thrown by Finn McCool from the top of a fort on a hill about a mile away and 'as we sat on it on summer evenings as children, it filled our imaginations. This was a real education, a deepening of the mind.' [16]

There were still local story-tellers living who kept alive the world of ancient mythology, and gave another dimension to many features of the local landscape. Slieve Gullion, which stood out so clearly against the skyline to the north-east, became in these stories a sacred mountain, a place of mystery. And in a cave near Ardee lay Garret Og with his horsemen, sleeping an enchanted sleep until the day he would come forth to save Ireland from her enemies.

Patrick Kavanagh contributed an essay entitled 'A World of Sensibility', to the dictionary compiled by his brother. In it he wrote:

The district in which I and the author of this book were born and lived our early lives was profusely rich in imaginative lore. Next to my home lived a great story-teller, Johnnie Cassidy. He died in 1956 though his father was born in 1800. He was a bridge back to a mythical past. [17]

The imaginative life of the people of Monaghan was not only fed on the remote past. There were still active ballad-makers in the district. One of them, self-styled 'The Bard of Callenburg', made up satiric rhymes about the local people.

Tailor Magrane putting in the long buck stitches
And Carpenter Hamil cutting his timber out of the ditches. [18]

At markets and fairs this bard would be offered drinks to make up rhymes about local affairs and personalities. He also appeared in print in the local newspaper, the *Dundalk Democrat*. Ballads of all kinds were popular at this time. Kavanagh remembered songs and ballads being sold in the small town fairs on coloured sheets of paper, and how people would read them out as they walked home from the station.

Kavanagh himself tried ballad-making while he worked. He got stuck in his first one because he tried to find a rhyme for unrhymeable 'Monaghan'. But some of his ballads were very successful.

17

They were useful ballads telling about football matches, dances, etc. More than thirty years later I heard one of those ballads being sung. It was about a wedding dance which a number of men tried to crash.

> Farelly climbed in by the window
> But Dooley fell back with a souse
> And the singing and shouting was terrible
> Round the halfbarrel of stout.[19]

Popular superstitions, story-telling and ballad-making — all these suggest that popular culture still belonged to an oral tradition. This was partly true, but there was also a good deal of reading, even in the country. 'When I was growing up,' Kavanagh remarked later, 'I remember that many people did read. And the books that were read were often good books — Carleton, Kickham, and Burns.'[20] The Kavanagh household itself contained very few books, but Patrick was able to borrow some from a neighbour and he found imaginative nourishment in the poetry of his schoolbooks, for which he always retained an affectionate regard.

The picture I have so far presented of the country world in which Kavanagh grew up seems a favourable, even a romantic one. But there was a darker side to it. In *Self-Portrait* Kavanagh laconically remarks: 'My childhood experience was the usual barbaric life of the Irish country poor.'[21] Although the Kavanaghs were more fortunate than some of their neighbours, they too lived in the shadow cast by poverty over the countryside as a whole. The 'big house' gentry were not numerous in Monaghan, but they were there, and at times the condition of the peasantry appeared akin to serfdom.

When I read Carleton I wonder if this serfdom didn't begin with the Great Famine. Carleton's farmers may be small but they were not beggars.

There was a big house in our vicinity, though if the truth were known the owners of that house were as poor as ourselves and trying to keep up a front. We called at the back door of the dilapidated big ruin for milk and other items and the poor devils handed out what they hadn't for themselves. I suppose that the important thing is to survive, that it's better to be mane than to starve.

Still, I feel somewhat embarrassed. I remember the foxhunt coming across our vast acres and saw with no little shame, young as I was, a middle-aged man rush up to the huntsmen and shout, "Who's the paymaster?" He got half-a-crown because he claimed to be the one who had directed the hunt towards the fox.

Although we were pretty bad in that area it was a sight better than being brought up in places like Meath. There was servility with a vengeance. A chap was telling me that when the gentry who owned this particular place went on holidays in the summer the three dogs used to make up to himself (a youth) and the butler. When the gentry came back the dogs cut the labourers dead. How terrible to be insulted by a pack of dogs.

I am not very politically or socialistically minded, yet I have strong feelings on these matters and I am sure that the men who went out in 1916 redeemed the honour of the common Irishman.

There were such things as ladies as distinct from women. "Don't you know that I'm a lady?" said one of these women to some schoolchildren who hadn't saluted. It was all quite ludicrous.[22]

One of Kavanagh's treasured books was a dog-eared copy of *The Sunlight Soap Almanac* for the year 1899. He was amused and appalled at the picture of the industrious poor presented in its pages, at a time when England was leading the world in industrial prosperity. The Almanac sets out a budget for a family of five living on 15/6 a week. It carefully explains how a young man can save a small sum each week by avoiding drink and cigarettes.

Thus in 8 years £36. 8. 0. may be saved by going without beer or tobacco. A lad who practices this small self-denial from 16 to 23 may in those 8 years save enough to furnish a comfortable cottage when he marries, for with the accumulated interest at $2\frac{1}{2}\%$ in the G.P.O. he will have amassed about £40.[23]

Kavanagh's brief comment is: 'The word "amassed" is good.'
In his later years Kavanagh was often to complain about the lack

of enlightenment and lack of adventurousness that seemed to blight the people he grow up amongst. He put the blame for this on poverty and poor soil.

No picture of country life among the little tillage fields of Monaghan would be complete without mention of the Roman Catholic religion that formed the ground pattern of all lives. The regular weekly attendance at Mass was a social as well as a religious occasion.

> Ah, well do I remember tripping along to Mass of a summer morning dressed in my new blue serge suit. And with a cap on my head that cost three and ninepence. Curious how the price of that cap stays in my memory. Ahead of me is a companion. When I catch up with him he remarks profoundly: "Great class of a morning." "A terror to the world," I equally profoundly reply. On the hills either side of the dusty road the crops are blooming. The priest flashed by in his round trap.
> "A wonderful pony that," I comment.
> "As fast as a motor-car."
> Gossiping women ahead of us and a row of middle-aged fellows stretched across the road, their heads before them, they taking long determined strides. . . . What makes Mass-going memorable is that it is done not idly but as a duty. . . . Outside the church men standing in groups talking about the weather, the crops or whatever comes into their dreaming minds. . . .[24]

Apart from the regular weekly attendance at Mass, there were, of course, the various festivals of the Church. Most notable were Christmas and Easter, and Kavanagh always remembered vividly the Christmases and Easters of his youth. One of the few poems of his earlier years that he felt able to enjoy and commend in later years is one describing the scene on Christmas Eve.

> I see them going to the chapel
> To confess their sins.
> Christmas Eve
> In a parish in Monaghan
> Poor parish and yet memory does weave
> For me about these folk
> A romantic cloak.

20

No snow, but in their minds
The fields and roads are white.
They may be talking of the turkey markets
Or foreign politics; but tonight
Their plain hard country words
Are Christ's singing birds.

Bicycles scoot by. Old women
Cling to the grass margin
Their feet are heavy but their minds flow
In dreams of the Mother Virgin
For one in Bethlehem
Has kept their dreams safe for them. . . .[25]

Writing in the *Irish Farmers' Journal* (1 April 1961) on 'The Wonder of Easter', Kavanagh again slips into verse as he recalls the Easters of his boyhood.

And I in my new suit of blue serge
And pointy, yellow shoes,
And well-oiled plentiful hair
Skip down the Mucker lane as teddy-boyish or beatnicky
As anything in today's news.

Patrick Kavanagh attended the local school, Kednaminsha and Rocksavage National School, where he was taught by a formidable Miss Cassidy, who used the rod freely. Here he made his first acquaintance with English poetry and he often recalled in later years the poetry of his school-books. He mentions Longfellow, Tennyson, Hood, Thomas Campbell, Thomas Moore, Whittier, Bret Harte, Cullen Bryant, R. L. Stevenson, Charles Kingsley, George Macdonald, William Allingham, E. Nesbitt and Gabriel Setoun. The school-children used to sing some of the popular poems to familiar airs. They sang 'Lucy Gray' to the tune of 'There's na luck . . .'. Years later Kavanagh still occasionally sang or recited these poems learnt at school.

I remember a delighted crowd in a bar listening to my rendering of —
Not a drum was heard, not a funeral note,
As his corpse to the ramparts we carried.[26]

21

It seemed to Kavanagh that other writers of whom he had read all had their origins in some literary background, but he felt that his own roots were in the school anthologies. As he walked or worked in the fields the words from these books echoed in his mind.

When I read —

> Often I think of the beautiful town
> That is seated by the sea

I am walking through a field called Lurgankeel away down towards a shaded corner. . . .

It is to the schoolbooks I must return for my virginal youth, for a winter morning in a desk near the fire, near the map of Scotland, with my head dipped into a new satchel sniffing the wonderful memorable smell of new canvas. . . .[27]

When Kavanagh left school he had no thought of becoming a writer. There were only two possibilities open to him: shoemaking and farming. He worked at both these trades, but without wholly committing himself to either. He once described himself as 'The Shoemaker Who Didn't Stick to his Last', and he confessed that he never really mastered the trade, in spite of his father's encouragement.

> I started to serve me time to the trade when I left school at the age of thirteen or a little more. My father said that I knew more about the trade than he did and that it was impossible to teach me — and he was right. In fact, in spite of my having spent about ten years at the business I never learnt how to make a welted boot.[28]

Although he never became a competent shoemaker, he retained an interest in the trade and its tools, and he often referred to it. One of the subsidiaries to shoemaking in the country was the paring of corns and he was often called upon to perform this delicate operation on the toe of a nervous old woman.

> "That'll do, you're going to bleed me."
> "Don't be worried, Maggie, I'm not near the pay yet."
> "Is it a soft corn?"
> "It's as hard as a grain of whate; an aisy job, Maggie." [29]

Kavanagh was more at home working on the land than he was at the cobbler's last, but he was not the kind of man to make a successful farmer. He was too much of a dreamer and, as he admits himself, 'a bit of a lazy bones'. Nevertheless he took a pleasure in many country tasks and a pride in his own strength and skill. He was delighted on one occasion in later years when one of his neighbours defended his former prowess from ill-informed sneers.

A fellow in a pub who wasn't treating me with the respect due to a top-class dung-filler, bag carrier and quarryman was told off by a bystander who said that not only would I have carried thirty stone of wheat up the thirty steps of the "Coiler's" loft, "but he'd carry a waster like you sitting on the top of it".[30]

Another neighbour recalls that he was not at all bad at ploughing. But the picture he gives of himself in *The Green Fool* suggests that his labour was not highly regarded by those farmers who hired him. And in the *Irish Farmers' Journal* he relates how he was sacked by Pat McCabe, 'the oul' slave driver'.

"You can go home. I'm paying ye twelve and a tanner a week, all found and I'd be in to pocket if I paid ye to stay at home. You ought to have been a preacher." [31]

In *The Green Fool* he tells the story of how he went to the old hiring fair at Carrickmacross and was hired by a farmer.* He seems to have done this partly in a spirit of adventure and because a companion urged him to join him. The story is corroborated by his words in *The Irish Press*, for which he wrote a personal column.

I once hired with a farmer. . . . Fifteen pounds he gave me for the half-year and a half-crown "earnest" there and then. He invited me into a public-house snug to take a drink of something (I was about fifteen years old at the time). I bolted from the snug when the half-crown was presented, for to take that was analagous to taking the Saxon shilling.[32]

---

*His accounts of hired labour seem to be fictitious. His brother Peter writes: 'None in our family ever went out for hire.' (*Lapped Furrows*, p. 9.)

Whatever his shortcomings as a farm labourer, Kavanagh did work on the land for many years. He used the plough and the harrow, the graip and the flail; he spread dung, thinned turnips, cleaned out ditches and sprayed potatoes. He gained an intimate knowledge of the fields and of country tasks, and he developed a love of them that is denied to those who merely look on as spectators. In later life he often recalled happy memories of the years he worked on the land. 'The happiest days of my life were the days when I was taking out the praties in a field called Cul an tsiopa — the back of the shop.'[33] He describes how they used a swing plough to throw out the drills of potatoes, which were then gathered into green baskets, loaded on to a cart and finally stored in pits.

> After tay I go down to the pits to have a last loving look.
> Very dry. There is a large full moon in the sky and I am young.
> So those potato digging days live in my imagination.[34]

But Kavanagh was not to remain among the potato fields of Monaghan. He was already writing poetry and reading books and magazines. New voices spoke to him from the pages of the *Irish Statesman,* and before long he was drawn to London and Dublin.

He came to London in May, 1937, just before the Coronation of King George VI, and spent some five months there. He was befriended by Helen Waddell, who took an interest in his poems and suggested his writing *The Green Fool.* He was also helped by John Gawsworth, a poet living in London.

At the end of 1939 he went to Dublin to make a living by his pen. He took a bed-sitter on the Drumcondra Road. 'There was a red sofa in my room. . . . I slept on a stretcher bed which cost 7/6. And there I was fresh and foolish from the happy country.'[35] He had a hard struggle to make a living. He refers to himself as 'a penniless buckaun in Dublin trying to make a living writing articles for newspapers. And the fees paid then. The maximum was a guinea and a half.'[36] He raised a few shillings by selling the books he got for reviewing to a second-hand bookshop. He also found a cheap cafe near Westland Row where he could get a nourishing lunch for 1/3: 'the best of fresh spuds and butter with some meat also. . . . It saved my life, living as I was on two pounds a week.'[37] He says in the introduction to his *Collected Poems* that he often borrowed a 'shilling for the gas' when he really wanted the money to buy a chop.

In spite of the hardship of these war years in Dublin he found a good deal of intellectual stimulus there, and he made friends. Through John Betjeman, then British Press Attaché in Dublin, he was invited to many big functions. He even played cricket for Sir John Mahaffy's eleven, in a charity match, where he had to face the bowling of Leary Constantine.

At this time the Palace Bar was the chief meeting place for writers and artists. Kavanagh recalled it in 1959, when writing his 'Memoirs of the War' in the *Irish Farmers' Journal*.

> The great intellectual centre was the Palace Bar, where Bertie Smyllie, the *Irish Times* editor held court. There really was a buzz on there which kept us from getting too sad. . . .[38]

Cyril Conolly, the editor of *Horizon,* visited Dublin in the war years and he described the Palace Bar in a special Irish number of the magazine.

> Irish society still puts an eighteenth-century value on wine, conversation or sport, kept apart from the women. Perhaps the one most remarkable male stronghold is the Palace Bar.
>
> The Palace Bar is a small back room in a pleasant tavern which is frequented entirely by writers and journalists; it is as warm and friendly as an alligator tank, its inhabitants, from a long process of mutual mastication, have a leathery look, and are as witty, hospitable and kindly a group as can be found anywhere. The Palace Bar is perhaps the last place of its kind in Europe, a *Café Litteraire,* where one can walk in to have an intelligent discussion with a stranger, listen to Seumas O'Sullivan on the early days of Joyce, or discuss the national problem with the giant Hemingwayesque editor of the *Irish Times.*[39]

The man from Monaghan was henceforth to spend most of his life in cities. Dublin was his centre, though he frequently stayed in London and he visited America and Europe. But his roots were still in Monaghan and the bulk of his writing both in verse and prose has for its setting the little tillage fields he had left. He often returned to Inniskeen and he sometimes bitterly regretted that he had not stayed there and continued farming.

If I had been true to myself and stayed put, not only would I have lived a comfortable rounded life and made money but if there is such a thing as Fame it would have walked in the gate of my home in the townland of Mucker. . . .[40]

But, for good or ill, he had by 1939 committed himself to the streets of cities and to life as a writer. There were temporary returns to the scenes of his youth, which changed as the years passed, but there was no final going back.

2

PORTRAITS OF THE ARTIST AS A YOUNG MAN

Kavanagh's articles in the *Irish Farmers' Journal,* and occasional articles in other magazines and newspapers, give many glimpses of his Monaghan background, but the fullest picture of his early years is found in his two books, *The Green Fool* and *Tarry Flynn.*

The Green Fool is written in the form of an autobiography and it gives an account of the poet's early years and the world he knew. The book begins with the child in his cot and ends with the young man's arrival in London. He gives real names to people and places, and a reader naturally assumes that he is reading a genuine autobiography. But later on Kavanagh referred to the book as a novel and he revealed that some parts of it were fictitious.

> I invented so many stories about myself in *The Green Fool* to illustrate my own unique character that I don't know myself what's true about me and what isn't.[1]

In chapter six, for example, he writes about making a religious pilgrimage to a holy well, Lady Well, on the fifteenth of August, the eve of the Feast of the Assumption, which is still observed as a day of pilgrimage in Ireland. Writing about this many years later, Kavanagh admits that he never in fact went to Lady Well.

> I once wrote about this pilgrimage and my alleged experience of going in a horse cart, but the truth is I never visited that holy well either by cart then or since. Though I often had a mind to go there to see how close to the reality my imagination was.[2]

No doubt there are other parts of the book where he is drawing on his imagination rather than his actual experience, but this does not really justify transferring the book from autobiography to fiction. Even if Kavanagh had not been on a pilgrimage to Lady Well, he must have heard a great deal about it from those who did go. The general picture of country life given in the book rings true. At first Kavanagh himself defended the truth of his own picture, though later on he was to reject the book as 'a stage-Irish lie'. In 1947 he reprinted an extract from it in the *Standard Easter Miscellany*, entitled 'Feasts and Feasts'. He added the following explantory note:

> I feel that I should write a note by way of explanation of the book from which this extract is taken. That *The Green Fool* is one of the truest books ever written is my claim. Truth in literature needs some explanation.
>
> A thing is not true in literature merely because it happened. A thing is true in literature when it could happen — to anybody. That is the basis of the trueness of *The Green Fool*.

This is good Aristotelian doctrine, and it answers sufficiently any doubts raised about the authenticity of his account of the pilgrimage to Lady Well. But later on Kavanagh repudiated the book with increasing animus. In 1958 another section from it appeared in the *Irish Farmers' Journal* under the title 'Haste to the Wedding'. This time his note is more critical.

> This article is extracted from *The Green Fool*, a novel I wrote twenty years ago and in which I tried hard to be entertainingly "Irishy". The description of a wedding has some whiffs of truth still, but mainly it recalls a way of living that is gone.[3]

Eventually 'Irish' became a dirty word for Kavanagh. In his resistance to a bogus 'Irishness' that the literary world seemed anxious to foist on writers in Ireland, he turned violently against his own book. In a note supplied to the Poetry Book Society Bulletin in June 1960, he makes his position clear.

> My misfortune as a writer was that atrocious formula which was invented by Synge and his followers to produce an Irish literature. The important thing about this idea of literature was how Irish was it. No matter what sort of trash it was, if it had the Irish quality. And that Irish quality simply consisted in giving the English a certain picture of Ireland. The English love "Irishmen" and are always on the look out for them.
>
> So it was that, in the sign of this horrible constellation, I

wrote a dreadful sort of stage Irish autobiography called *The Green Fool* (1938). I have never been able to live it down.

The book does not deserve the contempt with which Kavanagh treated it. The picture of the poet that we get from it is not at all that of a lepricorny, buckleppin' Irishman; nor is it true that the book in general exploits a 'stage-Irish' conception of country or people. There are some rather hackneyed romantic touches and a few soft patches that the later Kavanagh would have avoided. 'The secrecies of the good earth'; 'the hedges and whins where the fairy folk hide'; 'the flavour of a primitive world where men were simple and childlike and close to God': such phrases as these belong to literary cliché, to the facile 'Irish peasant' quality that some English readers may have expected, but they are no more than occasional lapses. Kavanagh, even at this stage of his life, was by no means such a green fool as he suggests. His romanticism is balanced by a shrewd ironic sense of the ridiculous. A passage of sentimental dreaming is quickly followed by the sharp edge of reality. For example:

> Standing on the top of one of my little hills one day in May I looked across at the sun-flecked plains of Louth and Meath and knew how fine a thing it was to be alive. The green fields and the simple homes and the twisty primitive folk told me of the unchanging beauty of Ireland. At my feet were primroses and violets, a magic carpet on which I could journey over the Baghdads of dreamland.
>
> In the hollow a man was hoeing potatoes. Now and then he would look my way and I knew he was slightly angry with me. He thought me a lazy good-for-nothing.
>
> As usual my reverie was violently disturbed by one of the men who appear so innocent at a distance, and at close range are savage godless creatures.
>
> "What the hell are ye dramin' about?" he shouted in a harsh voice.[4]

Kavanagh had a keen observing eye and ear, and the book has many revealing glimpses of country life and conversation. The sale of an ass seems a trivial and mundane event, hardly worth writing about, but he succeeds in giving it a lively interest and the conver-

29

sation of those engaged in the deal is both racy and authentic. It makes the dialogue of Synge seem literary and unreal.

The animal's owner was a thin, harmless-looking woman, her son was holding the ass's halter. The ass-dealers liked harmless-looking people. The dealer in this case was a square-headed young fellow, wearing on his face a stubborn stubble of about a month's duration. He had the woman's hand in one of his paws and his other open palm was poised.

"Here," he shouted, "ye'll take what I said."

"I said nothin'," the woman replied meekly.

He turned upon her a countenance composed of scorn and threats.

"Are ye tryin' to pull out?" he asked, and he at the same moment seized the ass by the halter.

"Let go that baste," the meek creature said with amazing firmness, "or if you don't I'll knock the grin of ye. If ye want to buy him straight and honest don't have any of yer hunker-slidin', for Mary Fallon is not the girl to stan' it."

The ass-dealer calmed down.

"There's no one in the world tryin' to take the wee baste from ye. Here, houl' yer hand." He struck the woman's open palm a great smack. "Thirty-bob," he said.

"In the name of the three gay fellas," the woman said, like one who had heard an incredible tale of evil, "in the name of the three gay fellas have ye no cuttin' up in ye to go bid me thirty bob for an ass that's worth five pounds."

The dealer looked at her and she looked back with equal eloquence. A crowd had gathered, but we were in the front row.

"What's between yous?" another man butted in. He was told. He looked at the woman and patted her on the shoulder. "This is a dacent woman I often had a dale with," he said, "and this a dacent man that's buyin'." He spread out his two hands and simultaneously seized the wrists of the buyer and the seller. Their hands both waggled like the hands of para-lytics; they wanted to show indifference.

"Listen to me, dacent people," the middle-man said, wagging his head, "yous will not break my word. Here let yous split the difference," and he slapped the pair of paralysed palms to unity.

30

"I sowl chape," I overheard the woman say to her son afterwards.

"Ah, well," the son replied, "I often heard da sayin' that ye were better be sarry for sellin' than sarry for not sellin'." [5]

The picture of country life as a whole that the book gives is clear-eyed and unsentimental. He reveals the meanness and suspicion, the 'vicious neighbourly hatred' that exists among the people. The malicious comment of a bystander at a wedding, when a bridgegroom of sixty is marrying a girl of twenty-one, is characteristic. 'She'll run the life outa him. Why, man, he won't be worth a second-hand chew of tobacco when he's after sleepin' a week with that one.' [6]

He describes how the neighbours react to illness, with a mixture of morbid curiosity and suspicion. When he was taken to hospital with typhoid fever the news soon spread.

"Mebby, Mrs. Kavanagh, with the help of God and his blessed Mother he might get well."

One neighbour-woman came in to make enquiries. She wanted to verify a rumour. As soon as she had it straight that I was bad she dashed across the hills to her brother with the news. It is only the bare truth to say that this pair were delighted. Their eyes said: "Isn't it great? Isn't it great?" "He busted himself," the brother said. The woman laughed. "I must be going," she said. There were other people who might not have heard of my illness yet and she wanted to get in the first telling. . . .

To be sick was a disgrace. People kept a case of sickness in the household quiet as long as they could. When it leaked out the people would say: "Now, aren't they close? Aren't they dubious minded? They must have the devil's bad opinion of the neighbours."

When anybody around fell sick it pleased us all. We whispered our profound medical wisdom.

"Would it be anything bad he has?"

"Yer not the first asked me that."

"Anything bad" usually meant venereal disease, and the sum of two questions as above was: — It surely is something

31

bad he has. Why should they be keeping it so close if it was only a pain in the head?

This secrecy regarding illness wasn't confined to human beings. If a cow or a horse was sick the neighbours only heard of it by stealth. You might see one of them peeping through a hole in the hedge, and hear the talk.

"Begod, that cow doesn't look good, she'll not over it, whatever it is she has."

If the cow died she would more than likely be buried during the night. The neighbours would miss the beast.

"What the divil happened to Brown's cow? Do ye think did they sell her?"

And it might be some woman would put the question directly to Brown's wife. "Did yez sell yon bracket cow, Judy?"

"Oh, we did to be sure," Judy Brown answers. "The jobbers came round and when the price was good we thought we'd be as well let her go."

"Well, in troth I heard she died on yez."

"Deed aye! The bad story is the quickest goes round. How is Peter's chist?"

"Peter, thank God, is grand, not the laste catch on him now."

"Isn't that the blessin'!"

When Judy Brown parted from her persecutor she went into the kitchen.

"Who was that ye had out there?" her man asks.

"Biddy Magee."

"A bad-minded article."

"She heard the cow died."

"Well, let her hear away. The cow's gone now and all our bad luck with her!"

"Amen." [7]

The Green Fool has considerable interest and value as a sociological document describing a way of life that has now passed away, but it is also a portrait of the artist. It records the making of a poet, and in spite of the fact that Kavanagh treats it as fiction it is interesting and revealing as autobiography. His tone varies, from a detached ironic objectivity — 'I was a bit of a lazy-bones, a bit of a liar and a bit of a rogue',[8] — to a slightly self-conscious assertion of his position as a poet.

32

'Though the coin of joy isn't legal tender in the mundane shops of the world, it is in the lands of Imagination, and I to-day, jingling my purse of memory, know I am richer than Rockefeller or Henry Ford or the Rothschilds ever were.[9]

But if we take the book as a whole he shows a clear-sighted understanding of his own development.

I think that one reason why he expressed such intense dislike of the book in his later years is that in it he accepts unequivocally, at times even exploits, his position as peasant poet. He speaks of his acute embarrassment in AE's drawing room at his hob-nailed boots and the patches on the knees of his trousers. But even in this early work Kavanagh is too honest a writer to present himself as a simple plough-boy poet. There is a play of irony and a complexity of tone and feeling that make it quite impossible to dismiss as a 'stage-Irish lie'. At times, indeed, the tone of the book is not unlike that of *Tarry Flynn*. There is the same rueful awareness of the contrast between the world the poet dreams of and the one he inhabits. There is a similar vein of rich comedy.

In a late chapter, 'Between Two Stools', he describes his divided feelings before he finally broke with the land. His poems had been published but he lingered in the country, feeling himself already a stranger within the gates. Some regarded him with fear and suspicion; others hoped to make use of his gifts.

On a Sunday afternoon as I sat in my room, a man called at our house: a man of about sixty-five, with a high blood-pressure bloom on his countenance.

"Does the poet live here?" he inquired when I went to the door.

I told him he was face to face with the poet.

"I'm glad," he said as I led him in. "I was afraid ye might be out."

He flopped to a seat and wiped the sweat from his brow with a red handkerchief.

"It's a very hot day," he said, "and I'm after walkin' ten miles."

"My goodness," I said.

He looked like a man who wasn't too sane.

"What can I do for you?" I asked.

33

"Ye can do a great deal for me," he answered. "I'm an unfortunate man livin' among the worst of bad neighbours; night, noon, and mornin' they have me persecuted. I want ye to make a ballad on them, a good, strong, poisonous ballad."

I was charmed. Here was a twentieth-century survival of the ancient faith in the power of the poet.

"I'll give ye the facts, and you'll make the ballad," he said.

"I'll make the ballad," I assured him.

He gave me the facts. He told me the names of his neighbours and their nicknames. He told me which of them had bastard blood in their veins and which of them had been accused of theft.

To be accused of stealing is in Ireland for a man a crime which most lowers him socially — it is worse than murder. For a woman, of course, the giving birth to an illegitimate child is a stain on herself and her family that will be revived in three generations to come.

"That should make the bones of a good ballad," the man said when he had finished. "What would you charge me for a ballad like that?"

This was sweet music. From the beginning of our encounter my only fear was that the fellow's obvious madness mightn't produce a reflex-action on the muscle-strings of his purse.

I tried to look as professional as possible.

"Ten shillings a verse I usually charge," I said.

I didn't like the look he gave me, the fire left his eyes which stared at me empty and unresponsive.

Perhaps I had asked too much.

"I'll do it for three pounds," I said. He shook his head.

"I might just as well go to a solicitor," he remarked in a melancholy tone.

"Well, how much yould you be prepared to give?" I asked.

"I though ye might do it for the price of a couple of bottles of porter," he said.

It was a big come-down for my pride. A couple of bottles of porter as remuneration for a poet. I dismissed my customer as gently as I could.[10]

Kavanagh has been one of the most unlucky writers in his

34

relations with law and authority. Sometimes he brought trouble on himself, as in the case of his ill-advised libel action against the *Leader,* which published an anonymous 'Profile' of him in 1952. (See page 89). But the publication of *The Green Fool* led to a libel action that must surely have come as a complete surprise to both writer and publisher. Dr. Oliver St. John Gogarty, the Irish poet and journalist, took exception to a sentence referring to his wife. In describing an early visit to Dublin, in search of the world of literature, Kavanagh told how he had called at Gogarty's house in Ely Place. He had been given the address at the National Library, where the assistant was unable to tell him the whereabouts of AE. A maid, or receptionist, in a white coat, answered the door, since Gogarty had a medical practice. Kavanagh wrote: 'I mistook Gogarty's white-robed maid for his wife — or his mistress. I expected every poet to have a spare wife.' [11]

It seems a little ungenerous of Gogarty to take a libel action over this fairly innocent remark, but he did so. The action, against Michael Joseph, Ltd., the publishers, was heard before Mr. Justice MacNaughton and a special jury in the King's Bench Division, London. Gogarty was asked by Counsel: 'Are you seriously inviting the jury to believe that the passage of which you complain meant that you were a person who might keep a mistress?' He replied: 'I did not like the word "mistress' being associated with my wife.' [12]

The jury, who had not seen the author of the book and did not know why he wrote it, returned a verdict for Gogarty and assessed damages at £100. Gogarty had never met Kavanagh. In *The Green Fool* Kavanagh records that he slipped away from the house as soon as the maid departed 'to see if the Doctor is in'. It is by no means certain that the incident ever took place since the book, as Kavanagh has insisted, is only fictional autobiography. Certainly it was an unlucky start to his adventure in publication.

The Green Fool presents a broad canvas of country life and it covers a wide span of years; *Tarry Flynn,** on the other hand, gives a close-up, in fictional form, of the local scene and of the poet's personality and predicament. It is narrower and sharper than the

---

Tarry Flynn was banned under the Censorship of Publication Act by a Prohibition Order dated 3 November 1948. The prohibition was revoked on 8 December 1948 by the Appeal Board.

earlier book and it gives a more detailed portrait of the poet, including his sexual tensions and his amorous daydreams. We see Tarry caught in the toils of the little tillage fields, ploughing and ditching, dreaming and writing poems, planning to seduce a neighbour's daughter, humbly adoring and clumsily repulsing the more distant Mary Reilly, daughter of a prosperous farmer. We also find him getting into trouble with the parish priest. At the end of the book he decides to leaves his native parish with his uncle, who is improvident and fond of drink, but vital and imaginative.

The chief characters in the book are Tarry himself and his mother. Kavanagh admitted that he was presenting himself and his own mother. In *The Green Fool* his mother remains a somewhat shadowy figure but in *Tarry Flynn* she stands out clearly and vividly, and her relationship with her son is more fully developed. She loves him deeply in spite of his queer and unsatisfactory ways and his 'curse-o'-God rhyming'. Her conversation has a racy edge. She nags sharply at her son when he is reluctant to leave for Mass:

> Lord O Lord! Aggie left here to go to Mass at five minutes to eight and there's that man still steaming away at the fag like a railway engine. . . . Oh look at him there with his big nose on him and the oul' cod of a face like his uncle that — that a Protestant wouldn't be worse than him. . . .[13]

Mrs. Flynn's tongue is not only sharp and lively in abuse. She frequently tries to encourage Tarry to ambition and independence. When there is a chance that a neighbour's farm may come into the market she says:

> And mind you, that's as dry and as warm a farm of land as there is in the parish. There's a couple of fields there and do you know what it is you could plough them with a pair of asses, they're that free. It's a terrible pity you wouldn't take a better interest in your work and you could be the independent-est man in Ireland. You could tell all the beggars to kiss your arse. . . .[14]

Much of the comedy and flavour of the book is derived from the contrast between mother and son. While Tarry writes poetry his mother prepares for her evening prayers.

Tarry took a candle and went upstairs to a corner of his bedroom and sitting on the edge of the bed took a writing-pad and began to write verses. Yards and yards of despair he wrote about his love for Mary Reilly.

> O God above
> Must I forever live in dreams of love?
> Must I forever see as in a glass
> The loveliness of life before me pass?

. . . The room was a typical country bedroom, its walls covered with holy pictures. Reading about artistic things Tarry had once suggested to his mother that they should take down all those ugly pictures. She thought him the most atrocious blackguard: "Is it them splendid pictures? Why there's three pictures there and the likes of them is not in the parish. I bought them second-hand and gave fifteen shillings apiece for them in Mick Duffy's last Easter was eight years. Troth and sowl they'll not be shifted while I'm here." . . . [a little later he hears her praying]
"Holy Mary, Mother of God, pray for us . . . cat, down out of that and don't be trying to lift the lid of that can . . . sinners now and at the hour of our . . . Tarry, come down out of that . . . death, Amen." [15]

Tarry Flynn shows more clearly than *The Green Fool* the growth of Kavanagh's semi-mystical love of nature. Tarry is vividly aware of the 'simple fantastic beauty of ordinary things growing'. The familiar earth around him, the nettles and grass and stones, are transfigured by his imagination and love.

> Every weed and stone and pebble and briar all along that ordinary headland evoked for him the only real world — the world of the imagination. And the rank smell of the weeds!
> What is a flower?
> Only what it does to a man's spirit is important.
> Something happened when Tarry looked at a flower or a stone in a ditch. . . .[16]

Tarry tries to tell his mother about his sense of wonder at the beauty of the fields. She is more concerned at the time with a corn she wants him to cut. The scene has something of the contrast between Don Quixote and Sancho Panza. Mrs. Flynn has a peasant shrewdness and her feet are firmly planted on the earth.

"Did you get finished?" said she.
"I did," he said. He organised his will for a remarkable statement. "The Holy Spirit is in the fields," he said in even cold tones. He was unemotional, for these statements did not lend themselves to any human emotion.
The mother who had one shoe off and her foot on a stool did not seem to have heard. "There's a curse o' God corn on that wee toe and it's starting to bother me again. I think we'll have a slash of rain. Get the razor blade and pare it for me." He held the foot between his legs like a blacksmith shoeing a horse. "Easy now," she cried, "and don't draw blood. Easy now, easy now. The Mission's operating next Sunday week, I hear. Aggie, run out and don't leave any feeding on the hens' dishes for Callan's ducks. Have you the pea out?"
"I have."
After a while she quietly asked:
"What was that you said about the Holy something?"
"I said the Holy Spirit was in the fields."
"Lord protect everyone's rearing," she said with a twinkle that was half humorous and half terror in her eye. She knew that there was no madness on her side of house — that was one sure five — but —
"Is it something to do with the Catholic religion you mean?"
"It has to do with every religion; it's beauty in Nature," he said solemnly but also dispassionately.[17]

The dry light of humour plays freely through the book, and Kavanagh shows that he can laugh at himself and his own awkwardness.
There is a continual ironic contrast between day-dreams and reality. Tarry's unsuccessful attempts at courting Mary Reilly are neatly pointed.

The conversation opened in the normal way:
"Hello."
"Hello, Tarry."

38

The way she used his Christian name fluttered Tarry's heart to little blown bits like leaves in a wind. Her voice caressed him.

"I wasn't expecting you," he said.

She just looked at him as she had looked once before, and he was quite helpless. But not completely. Automatically he said in a super-objective manner: "I was just thinking of going up this old road when you came —."

They walked, threading their way among the bushes and briars and over rabbit burrows and the greasy stumps of long-felled trees.

"Marvellous weather," said he with all the passion of a lover.

"Terrific," she said.

"Look at the rabbit," he said, continuing his love talk.[18]

There is something compulsive about a writer's pronouncements on his own work. When Kavanagh damns *The Green Fool* he puts those readers who like it in an awkward position; and when he praises *Tarry Flynn* for its 'uproarious comedy' [19] we are inclined to look first for this element in the book. We should remember D. H. Lawrence's advice to trust the tale, not the artist. There is some delightful comedy in *Tarry Flynn*, though 'uproarious' is not perhaps the first word that would have occurred to the average reader; but there is a great deal that is not comedy, and it is in many ways an unsatisfactory book.

A sharp corrective to Kavanagh's own high opinion of it is supplied by Mr. J. M. Newton in an essay on 'Patrick Kavanagh's Imagination'.[20] He gives quotations from the book to show 'how casually Mr. Kavanagh makes his assertions about Tarry's spiritual strength', and he finds 'a disaster at the novel's centre' in this failure to realise and embody more adequately Tarry's poetic insight. It is true that Kavanagh does frequently make rather flat and casual statements about Tarry's insight — 'he was able to see the wild and wonderful meaning in the commonest things of earth' [21] — and sometimes such statements come perilously near to cliché; but there is more support for such statements in the book as a whole than Mr. Newton allows. The many passages about Tarry walking and working in the fields, and his constant awareness of the beauty and enchantment of the earth, do have a cumulative effect that makes it possible for the reader to accept the writer's assertions. There is weakness rather than disaster in the portrayal of Tarry's poetic insight. The weakness is evident from time to time in the language, which becomes too obviously rhapsodic and exclamatory.

> O the thrilling daisies in the sun-baked hoof-tracks. O the wonder of dry clay. O the mystery of Eternity stretching back. . . .[22]
> O the rich beauty of the weeds in the ditches, Tarry's heart cried.[23]

A more important weakness in the book is the uncertainty of Kavanagh's attitude to his hero, a point which Mr. Newton also draws attention to. At times Kavanagh treats Tarry with ironic detachment, clearly seeing him in perspective, and the vision is often comic, as in the courting scene already quoted. But this scene does not end in comedy. Tarry's hesitation and his withdrawal from what he most wants, his lack of courage, is painful and pathetic. When the girl persuades him to sit down beside her,

> One part of his mind told him to run, that to be great he must run away from things like this. He knew it was fear, a deep instinct that he could never hope to hold this girl. . . .
> He had his hand on the bank behind her within one inch of her back. He would give a good deal to have the courage to move his hand one inch. Eventually he took his hand away altogether. . . .
> The girl had shut her eyes softly and was leaning her head towards Tarry. Tarry instead of yielding stiffened himself and she straightened up. . . .[24]

What does Kavanagh want us to think of Tarry's lack of courage? In general he seems to regard it as a kink, a natural misfortune. We are not encouraged to judge Tarry, in this respect at any rate. Moreover, as Mr. Newton points out, neither Tarry nor Kavanagh seem to see things for a moment from Mary's point of view. We are given no indication of how she might feel.

In a poem called 'Play', dated 1951, Kavanagh describes a scene

similar to the negative encounters of Tarry Flynn and Mary Reilly.
In a country lane in the early summer

> The hero of the play who is also the author
> Sits waiting for something to happen

When a beautiful girl arrives in the lane 'tall, full-bosomed', the
hero only makes comments on the weather.

> He does not act, he is imprisoned
> In the chamber of reflection
> He must go out and take an interest in people
> And not be the central character of the play
> If what happens to him is to be important
> It must be seen as the importance of others
> Bring in the girl and let her speak

The poem is an acute piece of self-criticism and one wishes that
Kavanagh could have revised *Tarry Flynn* in the light of it. But in
the novel he seems unable to 'bring in the girl and let her speak'.

Elsewhere in the book Kavanagh reveals an awareness of Tarry's
self-centredness and judges it.

> There was a defect in him which these secluded fields devel-
> oped: he was not in love with his neighbours; their lives meant
> little to him, and though off his own bat he was a very fine
> thinker and observer he had only one pair of eyes and ears
> and one mind. Had he loved his neighbours he would have the
> eyes, ears and minds of all these, for love takes possession.[25]

It would be wrong to wholly identify Tarry with Kavanagh. There
are times, as in this passage, when he stands back and makes
judgements; but the detachment is not maintained. Tarry clearly
thinks the thoughts and echoes the feelings of Kavanagh. Although
Kavanagh is aware of it he does not avoid self-pity. He is pitying
his own younger self.

> Oh God! if he could only transport himself down the years,
> three years into the future when all would be forgotten. The
> present tied him in its cruel knots and dragged him through
> bushes and briars, stones and weeds on his mouth and nose.[26]

In many ways autobiography suits Kavanagh's special bent

41

better than the novel. This explains why *Tarry Flynn* is less satis-
factory as a book than *The Green Fool*. Some of the uncertainties
of tone in it are due to a confounding of the two genres. Kavanagh
himself clearly felt somewhat unhappy about the form of the book.
An early version entitled *Stoney Grey Soil*, had something more of
a plot and was presumably less autobiographical in shape. I have
not seen this earlier version, but Frank O'Connor refers to it in an
article on 'The Future of Irish Literature' in the Irish number of
Horizon, issued in January 1942. The story told of an attempt
made by a group of girls and boys in the village to establish a
village hall where they could meet and hold discussions, an idea
which is opposed by the village tyrant, an ignorant good-natured
old parish priest. O'Connor writes:

> The hall is a symbol of the life they would really like to lead,
> but which they never can lead because the old village tyrant
> opposes the licensing of the 'Anti-Christ Hall', as he calls it,
> and there is no one strong enough to defeat him. And so we
> see the principal character, in love with a decent girl whom he
> can never meet under decent conditions, masturbating his soul
> away, until the girl he loves is seduced by the local Don Juan
> . . . while the hero settles down in comfort with a cow of a
> girl who has a little fortune, and the Anti-Christ hall becomes
> a cattle-shed.

Evidently Kavanagh became dissatisfied with this plot and removed it from the book. 'I eventually filletted the plot out of it
and left it a bit straggly.' [27]

In spite of the straggliness and the other weaknesses that I have
commented on, *Tarry Flynn* remains a book of considerable power
and achievement. Even if it is seldom uproarious, there is a great
deal of comedy in it, beautifully realised in racy and vivid dialogue,
as in the opening pages. The Flynns' quarrel with the Finnegans,
by no means all comic, has richly comic aspects, and so has Petey
Meegan's abortive attempt to make a match with Mary Flynn.* It

---

*It was the comic aspect of the book, and these scenes in particular, that
were portrayed most effectively in the dramatized version of *Tarry Flynn*,
made by P. J. O'Connor. The play was given 67 performances at the Abbey
Theatre and it received enthusiastic reviews.

may not be the *only* authentic account of life as it was lived in Ireland in this century, but it is certainly a wholly authentic and vivid account of one particular Irish world.

Kavanagh occasionally made references to other works of fiction and autobiography that he was engaged in writing, but he published no successors to *The Green Fool* and *Tarry Flynn*.* There are, however, a number of shorter pieces that should be mentioned. They provide further sketches, fragmentary but vivid, of the country world of his youth.

In *The Bell* for August 1951 there appeared 'Three Pieces from a Novel'. The first of these describes a local football match. The second records a vehement attack on religion delivered by a cobbler to a Bible-seller. The third, which is the most interesting, tells of an unusal and outrageous confidence trick. Peter McCabe buys a deserted public house for a small sum and sells it for a large sum to a stranger, by making it appear thriving and busy for one evening. The buyer, who soon discovers the truth, falls into a melancholy madness and finally commits suicide. It is a brief but powerfully ironic piece, and the sardonic humour reminds one of Carleton in some passages of his *Traits and Stories of the Irish Peasantry*.

He wrote again of football in one of his *Envoy* diaries. The game he describes is, of course, the Gaelic football that he himself played at Inniskeen. The piece is a vigorous and amusing description of the rough and tumble of the game, in which the passionate partisanship of local supporters plays a large part.

"Go on our Micky —"
"Gut yer man —"
"Bog him —" [28]

This sketch was later reprinted in a volume of *Irish Stories and Tales*.

Two more sketches of country life appeared in *X* journal in 1961 and 1962. 'The Flying Moment' recalls the time when he went to the station to fetch a load of coal, and 'The Cattle Fair' describes the ways of cattle dealers in Monaghan.

---

*Peter Kavanagh, editor of *November Haggard*, lists two novels of country life amongst his holdings of his brother's unpublished work.

All these fragments and sketches show that Kavanagh had a keen and accurate ear for the run of country conversation. This can be illustrated by an extract from 'Evocations of No Importance!' reminiscences that appeared in the last number of *Envoy* and reappeared in 'The Flying Moment'.

Why do you remember this particular part of the road so well? I know. Because this spot for no special reason reminds you of yourself going with your mother to the station of a Monday morning carrying the baskets of eggs and butter on the handlebars of the bicycle.

"And remember what I toul' you, to clane out them henhouses and whitewash the roosts. And don't forget to put the porringer on that wee calf and not have him sucking the other calf's nabel."

"Don't forget to bring me back John O'London's."

"If I think of it. There's Mary Foley ahead of us. I don't want to catch up with her for she'd pollute a person with her oul' talk about the wonderful man Cissie got. As far as I hear the devil the much he has, a few scabby acres in the wilds of Derryfanone at the back of God's speed where the devil shit the big needle. Might as well be transported. And there's another thing — for God's sake will you cut them nettles at the Meada gate, for they sting the legs of me every time I go out into the Meada. It wouldn't take you ten minutes."

"I'll do that."

"And you might if you have time tidy up that oul' haggard. But don't kill yourself. Don't try to take it all away in one graipful. Nothing for you only the lazy man's load. Go light and go often. Bad luck to her she's waiting for us. Good morning, Mary. I think we have loads of time."

"Well, now, I'm not so sure. Father Gillan passed me at little Bessy's and it can't be that early."

"We're safe enauff," says I, the scientific man. "The signal is not down for the up train yet. Once we get this far before the signal is down we are in bags of time."

"Patrick, you could nearly put Mary's basket on the carrier."

"Don't bother, sure it's not that heavy."

"It's a nuisance if you have a light basket, Mary. Give it to

him and don't be killing yourself. Good people's scarce and
bad people ought to try and mind themselves. Didn't poor
Micky Duffy go off very sudden? When I heard he was dead
and buried I couldn't believe me ears. I met him in the Carrick
fair — was it two months ago or three? I think it was around
April. When did we buy the drop calves, Patrick? Was it at
the fair or an ordinary Thursday?"

"Ordinary Thursday."

"The Lord save us and bless us but it's a sudden world.
But sure he has his family reared." [29]

There is a nice blend in this passage of the traditional phrase,
the familiar coin of country speech — 'at the back of God's speed',
'he has his family reared', — with the sharp flavour of his mother's
personal style and her sudden changes of focus in conversation.

Kavanagh has other claims on our attention; but no writer of
the twentieth century has caught more accurately and vividly the
tones and turns of Irish country speech.

3

A POET IN THE FIELDS

As Kavanagh himself has pointed out, when a young man ignorant of literary circles begins to write verse, he writes, not out of his innocence but out of Palgrave's *Golden Treasury*. I have already mentioned the deep impression made on him by the poetry of his school-books. Another early influence was the poetry published in local newspapers. A characteristic example, 'The Old School Clock' by John Boyle O'Reilly,* appeared in the *Dundalk Democrat* in January 1928. Kavanagh later recalled this poem with affection. Here is, the last verse:

> 'Tis the way of the world: old friends pass away
> And fresh faces arise in their stead.
> But still mid the din and bustle of life
> We cherish fond thoughts of the dead.
> Yes, dearly those memories cling round my heart
> And bravely withstand Time's rude shock:
> But no one is more dear or more hallowed to me
> Than the face of that old school clock.[1]

Poetry very rarely appeared in the *Dundalk Democrat*, but there was a regular verse corner in the *Irish Weekly Independent*, a Sunday newspaper, published in Dublin. Here Kavanagh's own verses first appeared in print in September 1928. In the next few months they appeared quite frequently and he records in *The Green Fool* that he began to receive fan mail from admirers of his verse. Many years later, referring to his early efforts, he remarked in *Envoy*: 'The bad verse I wrote was something atrocious.'[2] For once we can agree with his denunciation of his own work. Most of it was poor stuff; sentimental, worn poetic currency: 'mine eyes', 'faery lands', 'my sorrow-laden songs' and 'Nature has donned her shroud of sombre brown'. But the young poet was learning to make

---

*A poet and newspaper editor much respected in his time; born at Dowth Castle, Drogheda, in 1844.

verses and his later contributions show a marked advance. 'The Tramp Woman', published in February 1929, is distinctly above the general level of the verse corner. It did not win the prize for the week, but it was a better poem than the one that did.

> Night folded wings grey,
> Above the dark and the fair.
> She faded out of my day,
> I know not where.
> But fancy brings back to my mind
> A tramp woman rounding the wind.[3]

In the same month he had a longer piece accepted by the *Dundalk Democrat*.[4] It was entitled 'An Address to an Old Wooden Gate' and it was written in couplets, with some facility. Kavanagh quotes a few lines from it in *The Green Fool* but the complete poem is only available in the files of the *Dundalk Democrat*.* I quote it in full below so that the reader may better judge the great distance that separates it from Kavanagh's mature poetry.

It is amusing to find the youthful poet speaking in the voice of a time-worn sage and comparing himself to the dilapidated gate.

> Battered by time and weather, scarcely fit
> For firewood; there's not a single bit
> Of paint to hide those wrinkles, and such scringes
> Break hoarsely on the silence — rusty hinges:
> A barbed-wire clasp around one withered arm
> Replaces the old latch, with evil charm.
> That poplar tree you hang upon is rotten,
> And all its early loveliness forgotten.
> This gap ere long must find another sentry
> If the cows are not to roam the open country
> They'll laugh at you, Old Wooden Gate, they'll push
> Your limbs asunder, soon, into the slush
> Then I will lean upon your top no more
> To muse and dream of pebbles on a shore,
> Or watch the fairy-coloured turf-smoke rise

---

*It has now been published, together with other juvenilia in Peter Kavanagh's *The Complete Poems of Patrick Kavanagh*.

From white-washed cottage chimneys heaven-wise.
Here have I kept fair tryst, and kept it true,
When we were lovers all, and you were new.
And many a time I've seen the laughing-eyed
School-children, on your trusty back astride.
But Time's long silver hand has touched our brows
And I'm the scorned of women — you of cows.
How can I love the iron gates which guard
The fields of wealthy farmers? They are hard,
Unlovely things, a-swing on concrete piers —
Their finger-tips are pointed like old spears.
But you and I are kindred, Ruined Gate,
For both of us have met the self-same fate.

Kavanagh had not yet encountered the world of poetry beyond
the local newspapers; he had never heard of Yeats. But in the
summer of this year a chance encounter brought him into touch
with the Dublin literary world. He tells in *The Green Fool* how he
went to the Dundalk grass fair to sell four bags of grass seed, that
he had sieved and winnowed himself, and while he was there, he
bought an out-of-date copy of the *Irish Statesman*. It brought to
his eyes names he had never heard of before, such as Gertrude
Stein and James Joyce. It included a poem by Æ, the editor of
the journal, which Kavanagh quotes in *The Green Fool*.

> Paris and Babel
> London and Tyre
> Re-born from the darkness
> Shall sparkle like fire. . . .[5]

He says he hardly understood the poem, but it powerfully excited
his imagination. 'On that day,' he wrote, 'the saints of Ireland,
political and theological, lost a strong supporter. I never wrote for
the holy poets again.'[6] Many of the verses in the *Irish Weekly
Independent* were pious or patriotic, and piety and patriotism were
put before literary merit. Whether or not the saints lost a strong
supporter that day, Ireland certainly gained a new poet. Æ published one of Kavanagh's poems in October 1929 in the *Irish
Statesman* and sent him a guinea for it. It was the first poem that

he had been paid for and he always felt grateful to Æ for this early encouragement.

The poem was 'The Intangible', which is included in *Collected Poems*. It shows something of Æ's own influence in the semi-mystical belief in the unseen, the intangible. This is even more marked in the original version which ends with the lines, (omitted in *Collected Poems*)

> Two and two are not four
> On every shore.

Two more poems appeared in the *Irish Statesman* in February 1930. 'The Ploughman' and 'Dreamer'. Shortly after this the *Irish Statesman* ceased publication owing to an expensive libel action, but Kavanagh's poems were soon appearing in the *Dublin Magazine*. In 1936 his first collection, *Ploughman and Other Poems* was published by Macmillan in their series of Contemporary Poets.

The title poem, 'Ploughman', is representative of the poetry Kavanagh wrote at this period, both in theme and style.

> I turn the lea-green down
> Gaily now,
> And paint the meadow brown
> With my plough
>
> .   .   .   .
>
> I find a star-lovely art
> In a dark sod.
> Joy that is timeless! O heart
> That knows God.

This poem reveals a considerable lyrical skill, and a felicity of phrase, but is slightly self-conscious, and literary. One is aware of the influence of the Georgian pastoral mode in the strongly marked rhyme and rhythm and a deliberate simplicity. The poem does not escape sentimentality and the same weakness is found in several others in the collection. But glimpses of Kavanagh's honesty and intelligence are to be found even in this early volume. He can be ironic as well as wistful about country life. In 'Inniskeen Road: July Evening', he makes it clear that the simple contemplation of

49

nature is not enough. As he stands on the completely deserted road he thinks:

> I have what every poet hates in spite
> Of all the solemn talk of contemplation.
> Oh, Alexander Selkirk knew the plight
> Of being king and government and nation.
> A road, a mile of kingdom, I am king
> Of banks and stones and every blooming thing.

An early critic complained that the ephithet 'blooming' shocked the mind that had been 'wooed by sonnet grace'. But the line draws its force from the ambiguity of 'blooming', which both describes the vegetation and expresses neatly the poet's disgruntlement.

Another poem of this early period that shows how Kavanagh was finding a voice of his own is 'Shancoduff'.

> My black hills have never seen the sun rising,
> Eternally they look north towards Armagh.
> Lot's wife would not be salt if she had been
> Incurious as my black hills that are happy
> When dawn whitens Glassdrummond chapel.
>
> My hills hoard the bright shillings of March
> While the sun searches in every pocket.
> They are my Alps and I have climbed the Matterhorn
> With a sheaf of hay for three perishing calves
> In the field under the Big Forth of Rocksavage.
>
> The sleety winds fondle the rushy beards of Shancoduff
> While the cattle-drovers sheltering in the Featherna Bush
> Look up and say: "Who owns them hungry hills
> That the water-hen and snipe must have forsaken?
> A poet? Then by heaven he must be poor"
> I hear and is my heart not badly shaken?

This poem expresses a feeling for the countryside that is very different from the conventional pastoral sentiment that appears in many of the earlier poems. The face of Monaghan is accurately and lovingly revealed here and the image of the frost — 'the bright shillings of March' — is wholly original and not simply the traditional currency of pastoral.

Kavanagh did not merely look at these hills; he knew them intimately and worked in them, as the poem suggests. He owned some fields at Shancoduff, which was a prominent ridge of hills, crowned by an ancient fort or forth, about a mile from his home.

In 1942 Kavanagh published his most sustained and dramatic poem about Irish country life, *The Great Hunger*. There is a marked difference between this sombre and powerful piece of writing and the pastoral lyrics of *Ploughman and Other Poems*. It is not about the Irish famine of 1845 - 7, often referred to as 'the Great Hunger', but about the peasant farmer's hunger for life and love, frustrated by a narrow prudence and his bondage to the land. Patrick Maguire, the central figure of the poem, remains unmarried at the age of sixty-five, tied to his old mother and his little fields, 'a man who made a field his bride'. Readers who are unfamiliar with the special situation in rural Ireland during the latter half of the nineteenth century and the first half of the twentieth century might well wonder why a free man should remain a frustrated bachelor, when there were plenty of women available only too anxious to be married. The answer is to be found in the economic and social circumstances in Ireland after the Famine and after the land acts of the later nineteenth century. The latter gradually brought security of tenure to the peasant farmer, and finally gave him the ownership of the land he farmed. Before the Famine the Irish peasants had married early. Land was divided to provide a new holding, or new land was found that would serve to grow potatoes, the staple food. There was little incentive to enlarge or improve holdings because rents were likely to be increased and peasants had no security of tenure. As land became more important and peasants became owners, the pattern of marriage changed. A marriage became a very important economic transaction, not to be entered on lightly. A son might have to wait until his parents died and the farm was 'free' before he could bring home a wife to share it with him. A wife was expected to bring a dowry of land or cows or money, and this might also mean delay.

The result was that marriages became less frequent and much later. An economic historian sums up the position in these words:

In no other country whose statistics are available is the average age at marriage so high; in none is there so large a

51

proportion of life-long bachelors and spinsters. The farmer, single on the average until he is 38, is the Irishman latest to marry; and of farmers between 65 and 74 one in four is still a bachelor.[7]

Patrick Maguire is no solitary exception; although increasing prosperity is beginning to change the pattern of marriage once more, the figure of the lonely bachelor is still common in rural Ireland.

Kavanagh himself called attention to this aspect of rural life in *Kavanagh's Weekly*. In the fourth number he wrote a leading article on Crohan, a parish in the West of Ireland, where only one marriage had taken place in the course of a whole year. In another issue he comments on a breach-of-promise case, where both parties were aged thirty-nine. The defendant, who had given the plaintiff a gift of Rosary beads and promised that he would put the price of a good bullock in a ring, said that he couldn't afford to get married until his brother was made a Parish Priest.*

In his comment, Kavanagh makes the point, which is revealed more fully in the poem, that the pressures against marriage are not solely economic.

> I am strongly of the opinion that part of the reasons for the present conditions in rural parts comes from a moral — so-called — code that makes love and life impossible. If the impulse for life was properly strong it would burst these so-called moral walls as it has done in the past and wherever society is healthy. . . .[8]

The Great Hunger opens with a sombre picture of the mono-tonous toil of the potato-gatherers:

> Clay is the word and clay is the flesh
> Where the potato-gatherers like mechanised scarecrows move,
> Along the side-fall of the hill — Maguire and his men
> If we watch them an hour is there anything we can prove
> Of life as it is broken-backed over the Book of Death?

---

*In the files of the *Dundalk Democrat* I came across a similar case where the plaintiff was 45 and the reluctant wooer 'at least 60'. (4 Feb. 1922).

The gathering of potatoes had often been a happy experience for Kavanagh, but the hopelessness and frustration and narrowness of Maguire's life throw a shadow over his work in the fields.

> Poor Paddy Maguire, a fourteen-hour day
> He worked for years. It was he that lit the fire
> And boiled the kettle and gave the cows their hay
> His mother tall hard as a Protestant spire
> Came down the stairs barefoot at the kettle-call
> And talked to her son sharply: 'Did you let
> The hens out, you?' She had a venemous drawl
> And a wizened face like moth-eaten leatherette.
> Two black cats peeped between the banisters
> And gloated over the bacon-fizzling pan.

Time passes. Patrick promises himself marriage, but delays until it is too late. In a moment of insight he sees himself 'locked in a stable with pigs and cows for ever'.

> Who bent the coin of my destiny
> That it stuck in the slot?

Tied to his little acres and to his domineering old mother, there is nothing for him to look forward to but death, when he 'will hardly remember that life happened to him'.

> Patrick Maguire, the old peasant, can neither be damned nor
>   glorified;
> The grave yard where he will lie will just be a deep-drilled
>   potato field
> Where the seed gets no chance to come through
> To the fun of the sun
> The tongue in his mouth is the root of a yew.
> Silence, silence. The story is done.

The destiny of Maguire is tragic, in 'the weak washy way of true tragedy', but the poem is not merely a drab documentary of the potato fields. It presents a vivid and closely observed picture of life in an Irish country parish. Although Maguire is firmly pinned to earth, his feet in the dung and clay, there are times when he laughs and sees the sunlight and is aware of the Holy Spirit. He also has ordinary comforts and compensations: gossip and cards, and a

53

bob each way on the Derby. He goes to Mass on Sundays and attains the dignity of holding the collecting box at the chapel door. Kavanagh does not present only the dark side of country life, as George Crabbe does in *The Village*, and yet the tone of *The Great Hunger* is perhaps even more deeply anti-pastoral than that of *The Village*. The poem provides a sharp ironic antidote to nostalgic dreams of Irish peasant life, with a satiric side-glance at tourist admiration for 'the simpleness of peasant life'.

> The world looks on
> And talks of the peasant:
> The peasant has no worries;
> In his little lyrical fields
> He ploughs and sows . . .
> The travellers stop their cars to gape over the green bank into
>   his fields : —
> The travellers touch the roots of the grass and feel renewed,
> When they grasp the steering wheels again. . . .

Many critics and reviewers have given *The Great Hunger* pride of place among Kavanagh's poems, but Kavanagh himself did not like it. When the poem was broadcast on the B.B.C. Third Programme on 13th May, 1960, Kavanagh spoke a short introduction, explaining his view of it. He said :

> It is far too strong for honesty. . . . In places the poem here is a cry — a howl, and cries and howls die in the distances. . . . I will grant that there are some remarkable things in it, but free it hardly is, for there's no laughter in it.

Some years later, in his *Self-Portrait*, he referred to the poem again in similar terms :

> There are some queer and terrible things in *The Great Hunger*, but it lacks the nobility and repose of poetry.[9]

The burden of his self-criticism is that the poem is insufficiently detached and free — 'the real poetic compassion is detached' — to achieve the distance and the distilled effect of the comic spirit. He felt himself to be too personally involved in the poem. He is often a penetrating critic of his own work and he has put his finger on a weakness, even if he presses it too hard.

54

There is, of course, a personal involvement. Although at the time he wrote the poem Kavanagh had left the small fields of Monaghan for the streets of Dublin, and he is able to look at Patrick Maguire from a distance, objectively, yet at moments he is deeply involved and Maguire looks out with the eyes of Kavanagh.

> He stands between the plough handles and he sees
> At the end of a long furrow his name signed
> Among the poets. . . .

The poem has an edge of bitterness that springs from Kavanagh's own struggle against the tyranny of the plough and the fields. One of his poems published in the *Dublin Magazine,* but not included in *Collected Poems,* makes clear this personal struggle and resentment.

> Plough, take your thin arms from about my middle
> Leave me free to unscroll the wisdom of other flesh.
> Ah, you are jealous, plough, you drive the fingers
> Of your lust-longing deep in my folds of manhood.
>
> Release me, release me, my desires would run
> In shallower furrows of passion. I am no Christ.
> Your breath is too strong. You hurry me towards
> A monument-immortal cowardice.[10]

Maguire found no release. He remained 'locked in a stable with pigs and cows forever'. Kavanagh broke free, but his spirit retained the marks of struggle, the memory of the 'tortured poetry' written by 'the pulled weeds on the ridge'.

The lack of repose in the poem which Kavanagh later detected is related to his personal involvement, but if this is a source of weakness it is also a source of strength. Kavanagh writes from inside the world of the little fields; he is not just looking over the bank from the roadside like the motorists he refers to, and like some other poets of the countryside.

There are undoubtedly weaknesses in the poem; there is a raw edge now and again, a certain stridency that sometimes grates on the ear; but taken as a whole it is profoundly moving. Although there are occasional lapses when the vitality of rhythm and language seems to flag a little, for the most part the writing is taut and resonant, and it combines a colloquial ease with flashes of vivid imagery. Kavanagh catches brilliantly the turns and tones of country talk and reflection. There is the card game, for example, or this picture of Maguire at Mass:

Maguire knelt beside a pillar where he could spit
Without being seen. He turned an old prayer round:
'Jesus, Mary and Joseph pray for us
Now and at the hour of our death. . . .
Wonder should I cross-plough that turnip ground?
The tension broke. The congregation lifted its head
As one man and coughed in unison.
Five hundred hearts were hungry for life —
Who lives in Christ shall never die the death.
And the candle-lit Altar and the flowers
And the pregnant Tabernacle lifted a moment to Prophecy
Out of the clayey hours.
Maguire sprinkled his face with holy water
As the congregation stood up for the Last Gospel.
He rubbed the dust off his knees with his palm, and then
Coughed the prayer phlegm up from his throat and sighed:
      Amen.

There is a fine control of pause and flow in the verse here. The fifth line suggests the quick snatch of mundane thought. After the short statement, 'The tension broke', the verse flows easily towards the climax in 'Out of the clayey hours'. The movement changes again with the relaxation of the next line, and throughout there is a delicate play of irony in the balance between the clay and the prophecy in the mind of Maguire.

In his preface to the *Collected Poems* Kavanagh complains that '*The Great Hunger* is tragedy and Tragedy is under-developed Comedy, not fully born'. He was making the same point when he complained, in his B.B.C. introduction that 'there's no laughter' in the poem. Kavanagh's characteristically sweeping aphorism about tragedy being underdeveloped comedy is worth pondering, but I find it impossible to accept as a valid generalization. There are inevitably tragic moods and modes that are not developing towards comedy. We might equally well complain that there is no laughter in *The Waste Land;* the pub scene in section II may arouse laughter, but it is mocking, ironic, hardly in the spirit of comedy. Like

The Waste Land, though in a very different setting, *The Great Hunger* depicts frustration. Indeed there are a number of significant poems in the twentieth century that could be called studies in frustration. To what extent they were fathered by Eliot it would be difficult to say. There is no direct relationship between Prufrock, or the protagonist of *The Waste Land,* and the pathetic figures of Maguire, Morgan and Martha Blake, for example, but they are all inhabitants of a twentieth century waste land. The influence of Eliot's moods and attitudes is felt in places far remote from his 'unreal city' of London. At the same time Maguire and Morgan have more in common with each other than either has with Prufrock. The Reverend Elias Morgan, B.A., is the puritan pastor of a remote hill parish in Wales. He is the central figure in R. S. Thomas's poem *The Minister.* There is no laughter in this poem, either; it tells of a land

> where men labour
> In silence, and the rusted harrow
> Breaks its teeth on the grey stones.

Morgan, like Maguire, though for different reasons, is one of those

> Condemned to wither and starve in the cramped cell
> Of thought their fathers made them.

In *Martha Blake at 51* Austin Clarke writes of the pathetic death of a pious spinster who formerly attended early Mass every morning. She dies in a hospital run by nuns.

> Unpitied, wasting with diarrhoea
>   And the constant strain,
> Poor Child of Mary with one idea,
>   She ruptured a small vein,
> Bled inwardly to jazz. No priest
>   Came. She had been anointed
> Two days before, yet knew no peace:
>   Her last breath, disappointed.

Clarke's poem expresses the pathos of silently endured frustration, illness, loneliness and death; but its scope is much narrower than that of *The Minister* or *The Great Hunger. The Minister* has three characters and a narrator; it was designed for broadcasting.

57

It has much in common with *The Great Hunger*. Both poems create a rural world, but their tone is strongly anti-pastoral; both stress the harshness of nature and the stunted lives of the labourers. In Thomas's poem the chapel and the words of Christianity are ineffective in the context of the bleak moors

> love's text
> Is riddled by the inhuman cry
> Of buzzards circling above the moor.

In Kavanagh's poem life 'is broken-backed over the Book of Death' and Maguire ploughs against a cold black wind blowing from Dundalk. But the little tillage fields of Monaghan are less harsh than the bleak hill country of Wales; it is fear of the Lord and ignorance that combine with the fields to give Maguire 'the coward's blow'.

The Great Hunger has a wider range, is more varied and complex in form and rhythm and tone than *The Minister,* which has the force of concentration on a single mood. Although the main theme of Kavanagh's poem is the frustration of the body and spirit of Maguire, yet he does create a whole parish around his central figure. We are aware of scraps of gossip and conversation. Maguire is not an unsocial man; he joins in the talk at the crossroads and he plays cards. When Kavanagh complained that the poem was too much a howl and a cry he was unjust to his own work. It is not more of a howl than Brian Higgins's poem *The North,* which gives a grim and negative picture of the industrial northern cities. The sense of frustration is certainly no stronger than that we find in *The Waste Land*.

Much of the horror and disgust at the civilisation and the people of Eliot's 'unreal city' springs from his treatment of sex. There can hardly be a sexual encounter in literature more repellent and chilling than the seduction of the bored typist by the young man carbuncular in 'The Fire Sermon'. The damning up of the natural flow of love and sex is at the centre of the frustration in Kavanagh's rural waste land. But Maguire's self-abuse —

> Pat opened his trousers wide over the ashes
> And dreamt himself to lewd sleepiness

seems less repellent than the sterile and unloving encounters of Eliot's hollow men and women.

The Great Hunger may also be considered as a 'pastoral' poem of the twentieth century, depicting a rural life that has already largely vanished. It has been linked with *The Deserted Village*, but there is very little in common between Goldsmith's nostalgic dream of 'sweet Auburn' and Kavanagh's stern picture of Monaghan. We get an equally strong contrast if we set *The Great Hunger* alongside Wordsworth's *Michael*, another 'pastoral' poem with a lonely, suffering man as its central figure. Michael's suffering is due to a single misfortune falling on him in his old age. Apart from this, his life is one of humble dignity and content. He is idealised as a noble peasant, a shepherd in daily contact with the uplifting presences of nature.

> And grossly that man errs, who should suppose
> That the green valleys, and the streams and rocks,
> Were things indifferent to the shepherd's thoughts.

Wordsworth does not call our attention to the dung and the clay that cling to the feet of peasants; he ignores the boredom and the ignorance, the meanness and lust that Kavanagh makes us keenly aware of. This is not to say that Kavanagh is simply a dreary 'realist', disillusioned and sour, and anxious to explode the myths of pastoral innocence and beauty. On the contrary, it is his keen awareness of the possibilities of life and love and the light of the imagination that makes him aware of the frustration and misery of Maguire's restricted lot. Indeed Maguire himself has intimations of immortality, glimpses of joy and eternity. He is no more indifferent to nature than Michael is, but his response is less steady and dignified, dragged down by practical and personal cares. He and his fellows are still keenly aware of sunlight and flowers and the rising sap in springtime.

> Yet sometimes when the sun comes through a gap
> These men know God the Father in a tree:
> The Holy Spirit is the rising sap,
> And Christ will be the green leaves that will come
> At Easter from the sealed and guarded tomb.

Wordsworth's single-mindedness in *Michael* is reflected in the grave dignity and simplicity of his blank verse, quietly even in tone and diction from start to finish. Kavanagh ranges through a variety of tones and rhythms, from the Biblical-prophetic opening —

Clay is the word and clay is the flesh

to the jazzy repetition and colloquialism of

Sitting on a wooden gate,
Sitting on a wooden gate,
Sitting on a wooden gate
He didn't care a damn.

Whether we see it as a twentieth century descendant of English pastoral poetry, or a rural 'waste land', it seems to me that *The Great Hunger* is a major poem and Kavanagh's own repudiation of it should not prejudice the reader's judgement. Although Maguire is a small peasant farmer in an Irish parish he takes on a universal significance. He is typical of many men who lead lives of quiet desperation. He has some awareness of his own condition but he lacks the insight and the courage to act from the promptings of his deepest feelings. In spite of this he is not insignificant or contemptible, and Kavanagh does not despise him, nor does he condescend towards him. There is pity for his fate but it is saved from sentimentality by irony. He writes with profound sympathy because he himself has been in Maguire's situation, but also with detachment because he writes as a poet. The 'ordinary barbaric life of the Irish poor' has found a new voice, sombre, powerful and haunting.

The publication of this poem brought more trouble to Kavanagh, but the trouble was not as serious as rumour has suggested. Some exaggerated statements have gained currency about the prosecution and seizure of the poem when it first appeared. The facts, as far as I have been able to discover them, are as follows.

The first section of the poem was published in an Irish number of *Horizon* in January 1942, under the title of 'The Old Peasant'. This contained the first three and a half of the final fourteen sections of the poem. Someone in authority evidently took exception to the second section which refers to Patrick Maguire's habit of masturbation. Two policemen called on Kavanagh at his lodgings and questioned him about the offending lines. 'We had a talk about Chaucer. They didn't know much about him,'[11] Kavanagh drily commented. This incident has been greatly exaggerated. John Ryan, writing in generous indignation described it as 'an ordeal for which history would have to be ransacked to find an equal,' [12] and recounts how special police agents and the Minister of Justice bullied the author and how his landlady, alarmed by the police visits, ordered him to quit.

The Great Hunger was published in full, including the offending lines, by the Cuala Press in April, 1942, and no action was taken against it. Mrs. W. B. Yeats, who was in charge of the Cuala Press at that time writes:

> The Cuala Press edition was not "banned on publication by a special exclusion order of the Minister of Justice". The Cuala Press edition was sent to all the usual subscribers and as *"Horizon"* had been confiscated by the Customs I sent 100 copies — which had not been subscribed for — to a London bookseller in case there should be any trouble about the Cuala Press edition. I do not think there would have been any trouble, but my co-editor F. R. Higgins who was a timorous person thought "the police" might descend on the Press!! [13]

It is difficult to establish exactly what did happen to the January number of *Horizon* in Dublin. The Customs authorities did not confiscate it, and it appeared in the bookshops. The police have no record of any seizure, but from the evidence of all those who remember the occasion there is no doubt that copies of the magazine were confiscated.

When *The Great Hunger* was published in the collection entitled *A Soul for Sale* (Macmillan 1947), the offending lines were omitted, but they were restored again in the *Collected Poems*.

The last word is with Kavanagh himself. He says in the author's note to the *Collected Poems* that the police were right. 'There is something wrong with a work of art, some kinetic vulgarity in it if it is visible to policemen.'

In June, 1942, Kavanagh went on a pilgrimage to the famous holy island of St. Patrick in Lough Derg, Co. Donegal. He had already visited it in 1940 but he went again in 1942 to refresh his memory and he wrote an article on it for the *Standard*. In this article he sees in Lough Derg 'a challenge to modern paganism' and it impresses him with the 'freshness and recency of Christianity'.[14] But his brother Peter reveals that his motives for going there were by no means purely religious.

> Patrick had no pious intent in going there. A book by him on Irish Pilgrimages, he thought, might be a best seller. Ten years later he still had the idea, and Hollis and Carter, Publishers, advanced him two hundred pounds on the unwritten book.[15]

The book on Irish Pilgrimages was never written, though Kavanagh did contribute some articles to the *Standard*. But in 1942 he wrote a long poem entitled 'Lough Derg'. This poem remained unpublished until his brother printed it in *November Haggard* in 1971. Although it has rough edges and seems unfinished in places— some passages are more like notes for a poem than the completed verse — it is a poem of real power and originality. One wonders why Kavanagh never published it. There is an uncertainty of tone and a divided vision in that he may have felt unable to resolve. As Brendan Kennelly put it succinctly to me 'He doesn't know whether he's on his knees or on his feet'. In a letter to his brother he seems inclined to dismiss the whole idea of pilgrimage and penance as a 'pious lie'.

> Lough Derg is typical of what may be called the Irish mind. No contemplation, no adventure, the narrow primitive piety of the small huxter with a large family.[16]

But in the poem this contempt is only one strand in a complex pattern of thought and feeling. Perhaps 'pattern' is the wrong word to use. The poem is like a documentary film in which the director is not yet sure of his standpoint and intention. Kavanagh mocks the pilgrims who come from motives of narrow provincial piety, whose 'hands push closed the doors that God holds open'.

> Solicitors praying for cushy jobs
> To be County Registrar or Coroner,
> Shopkeepers threatened with sharper rivals
> Than any hook-nosed foreigner.
> Mothers whose daughters are Final Medicals
> Too heavy-hipped for thinking,
> Wives whose husbands have angina pectoris,
> Wives whose husbands have taken to drinking.

But Kavanagh is aware that there are some pilgrims who rise above the narrow rut of materialistic piety, whose real religious needs evoke a response from the island. A humble grocer from Castleblayney, for example, finds himself moved to write words that carry him beyond the range of his own everyday understanding. Religious emotions are not the only ones felt on the island of purgatory. In 'the prayer-locked multitude' there are individuals nursing their private hopes and dreams with little reference to St. Patrick. One of them, 'A half-pilgrim who hated prayer', finds his love and longing awakened by a woman's face. Red-haired Robert Fitzsimons sees Aggie Meegan in the Sexton's kitchen and realises that he wants her. Later he talks to her ponderously, philosophically, while she only wants to hold his hand. He speaks with 'the naiveté of a ploughman' and reminds us of Tarry Flynn 'courting' Mary Reilly. For a moment it seems as though the poet might half-identify himself with Robert Fitzsimons and put him at the centre of the poem, but his story is hinted at rather than developed. Aggie tells Robert, as they sit on the wall of Brendan's cell, her dark secret of 'Birth, bastardy and murder'. He is appalled and broods all day over her terrible sin, until in the evening

> the green tree
> Of humanity
> Was leafing again
> Forgiveness of sin.

Robert promises Aggie that he will never reveal what she has told him and then the episode fades into the ending of the poem. The story is told only in scattered fragments, between descriptions of other pilgrims and glimpses of the routine of prayer and piety that continues on the island.

Kavanagh's complaint about *The Great Hunger*, that it had some queer and terrible things in it, but lacked the nobility and repose of poetry, applies more truly to 'Lough Derg'. If there is little laughter in *The Great Hunger* there is even less in 'Lough Derg'. It lacks the unity and consistency of *The Great Hunger*, where the figure of Maguire provides a central hub round which the spokes of parish life radiate. There is no firm centre in 'Lough Derg' and the poet's own attitude and his relation to the other characters, remains shifting and uncertain. The poet includes himself in the poem, but his position is indeterminate.

> The poet wrote it down as best he knew
> As integral and completed as the emotion
> Of men and women cloaking a burning emotion
> In the rags of the commonplace, will permit him.
> He too was one of them.

These lines are a somewhat naive excuse for a poem that is not fully integral and completed. The tone and versification here, with the rather clumsy repetition of the word 'emotion', are characteristic of a poem that has a rough-edged, unfinished quality, as though the poet were simply making use of his notes or his diary.

But even when these limitations have been fully acknowledged the poem retains a sombre power and beauty. There are keen flashes of observation:

> A Leitrim man
> With a face as sad as a flooded hay-field,
> Leaned in an angle of the walls with his rosary beads in his
>   hands.

The routine of the island, the coming and going of the pilgrims, is vividly caught in these lines:

> The bell brought the sleepers from their cubicles.
> Grey-faced boatmen were getting out a boat.
> Mass was said. Another day began.
> The penance wheel turned round again.
> Pilgrims went out in boats, singing
> "O Fare thee Well, Lough Derg" as they waved
> Affection to the persecuting stones.

The poet finds boredom and meanness and 'the narrow primitive piety of the small huxter' on the island of St. Patrick, and he feels like screaming at mediocrity. But at the same time he is able to enter imaginatively into the hearts of many of the pilgrims and he presents their prayers with a deep pity and sympathy. This is found in the four prayers 'shaped like sonnets', one of the most moving sections of the poem. One of the sonnets is a young girl's prayer to Saint Anne.

Saint Anne, I am a young girl from Castleblayney
One of a farmer's six grown daughters.
Our little farm, when the season's rainy
Is putty spread on stones. The surface waters
Soak all the fields of this north-looking townland.
Last year we lost our acre of potatoes
And my mother with unmarried daughters round her
Is soaked like our soil in savage natures.
She tries to be as kind as any mother
But what can a mother be in such a house
With argument going on and such a bother
About the half-boiled pots and unmilked cows.
O Patron of the pure woman who lacks a man
Let me be free I beg you, St. Anne.

4

THAT CHILDHOOD COUNTRY

'We make out of the quarrel with others, rhetoric, but of the quarrel with ourselves, poetry',[1] wrote Yeats. One part of Kavanagh's quarrel with himself had its origin in the 'stony grey soil' of Monaghan. Must he love it or hate it? At the end of his brief introduction to the B.B.C. broadcast of *The Great Hunger* he said that the life lived in the society and the landscape described in the poem was still 'sad, grey, twisted, blind — and just awful'. This is not the picture of Monaghan that he paints in *The Green Fool* or even *Tarry Flynn*. The words have a tone of bitterness that is never revealed in his country reminiscences in the *Irish Farmers' Journal*. They serve to indicate the ambivalence of his feelings towards the countryside where he lived and worked. From this tension of opposites much of his poetry is derived.

He remarked in *Envoy*: 'The only places fit for a writer to live in are cities.'[2] In his *Self-Portrait* he referred bleakly to his childhood experience in the country, and he frequently complained about the lack of enlightenment, the 'fog of unknowing' that enveloped him in these early years. In a broadcast on Radio Eireann given in 1941, entitled 'Looking Back', he said that the worst feature of being brought up in a backward country place was the slowness of the mind's growth there — 'or rather not so much the slowness of its growth as the slowness of its coming awake'. He attacked the myth about the value of 'roots in the soil' and the belief that there is freshness of thought and freshness of language in the country.

> In one day in a country place you will hear as much cliché language straight from the cheapest type of Sunday newspaper, as many American wisecracks and more jazz than in a year on Grafton Street.

> Even fresh fish and fresh vegetables are more readily available in the city than in the country. The idyllic vision of life in the country places of Ireland is simply a day-dream.

66

Whenever I look at that place (his birthplace) realistically I see it in an evil light. The sucking away of life, the very essence of men, till they are old and grey and full of sleep.

But even in this talk he admits that there is another side to the picture. He recalls with pleasure memories of threshing and 'the romantic smell of steam engines'. He suggests that the slowness of coming awake in the country may be a good thing for a writer who can grow with 'that peculiar slowness which in the end catches up and passes the weak sharp and short gallop of the university graduate of talent'.

The dualism of Kavanagh's feelings about the countryside continues through all his work. Golden memories of Christmas and harvest, and the spell of familiar place-names, must be set against bitter attacks on the backwardness and barbarity of the country. But in the dialogue of love and hate it is love that finally predominates. This is perhaps especially true of his poetry. There are very few poems that express the resentment against his country upbringing that is sometimes found in his prose comments. One of them is 'Stony Grey Soil' published in *A Soul for Sale* (1947).

> You flung a ditch on my vision
> Of beauty, love and truth.
> O stony grey soil of Monaghan
> You burgled my bank of youth.

Even in this poem the hate is mingled with love. We are aware of it in the catalogue of place names — 'Mullahinsha, Drummeril, Black Shanco'. Hate is sometimes only the reverse side of the coin of love. Kavanagh himself points this out in some characteristically pointed and perceptive words about the nature of art.

> The artist may hate his subject with that kind of furious enthusiastic hate which is a form of love, and which equally with love is a giver of life in literature. But when he dismisses it with contempt he is guilty of the sin against the Holy Ghost.[3]

He records the conflict of his feelings about the Monaghan countryside in an article he wrote for the *Standard* entitled 'Sunday in the Country'.

> All last week I argued with my mother and my friends

against the quality of living which is possible in this poor tillage country. We attack what we love. Nothing profound about that, for love is an enslavement, an irrational thing against which we hold out as long as we can. But surrender is happiness.[4]

In *A Soul for Sale,* and indeed in the poems as a whole, it is love and surrender that are most apparent. Many of the poems about his childhood country were written when he was living in Dublin or London. The following passage from his *Envoy* diary reveals the mood from which the poems sprang.

On this breezy October day sitting looking out of a window in London, I am vividly back in a small potato field, turning out the drills of potatoes. Unconscious. Didn't know my age. And the yellow briar leaves with holes in them and the pock-marked poplar leaves and the dry clay and the wonderful appetite it gives. O love.[5]

Kavanagh's quarrel with himself over his country background was complicated by friends and critics. Although he once saw himself as 'the green fool' (the Irish peasant poet) he passionately resented being labelled and stereotyped in this role. Indeed all his life he fought an uphill battle against the literary and journalistic label. He resented being 'exhibited as a strange animal discovered by a visiting journalist'.[6] He uses these words in an indignant letter to the *New Statesmen* in 1949, after 'Critic' had described him as playing the part of a stage Irishman and being a natural poet, the poet of the plough.

How was he to shake off the offending and falsifying stereotype while remaining faithful to the childhood country that he loved? He strenuously resisted the popular image of the poet, especially the Irish poet, as 'an inspired idiot': and the 'fallacy that because a man is born in the country his sensibility and feeling for life deserts him when he leaves his green fields'.[7]

One of his most successful poems springs from the attempt to re-affirm his love of the country while resisting the stereotype. In the *Bell* he describes his poem 'Innocence' as 'an answer to some superficial or vicious people who would have me cornered in a

small field';[8] and elsewhere he called it 'my reaction to the idea of
the inspired country idiot'.[9]

> They laughed at one I loved —
> The triangular hill that hung
> Under the Big Forth. They said
> That I was bounded by the whitethorn hedges
> Of the little farm and did not know the world.
> But I knew that love's doorway to life
> Is the same doorway everywhere.

> Ashamed of what I loved
> I flung her from me and called her a ditch
> Although she was smiling at me with violets
> But now I am back in her briary arms
> The dew of an Indian Summer morning lies
> On bleached potato-stalks —
> What age am I?

> I do not know what age I am,
> I am no mortal age;
> I know nothing of women,
> Nothing of cities,
> I cannot die
> Unless I walk outside these whitethorn hedges.

This poem, published in the *Bell* in November 1951, is one of a
group of what might loosely be called Monaghan poems. Some of
them are included in *A Soul For Sale*, others not. They show us
one side of Kavanagh's achievement as a poet, his own distinctive
and personal kind of nature poetry. Before examining them more
closely, I would like to consider further his particular approach
to his natural surroundings.

Kavanagh, unlike many other Irish writers, did not leave his
native fields never to return. In later years he returned many times
to Inniskeen and his comments reveal the continuing tension of
opposites. His returns were both joyful and saddening: he felt both
continuity and separation, sameness and difference. His changing
moods are reflected in his articles in the *Irish Farmers' Journal*.
A return visit at the end of October 1958 brought him deep
happiness.

"Indian Summer in the forest, it is years since I knew such peace." . . . I felt like the character in Knut Hamsun's beautiful novel of wandering in the Norwegian forests when I stayed in my home fields for four days. . . .

Indian Summer was over the little hills. And as I stood outside in the dusk the spirits of the past came alive in my imagination, and I realised that ghosts are real though possibly invisible. I was indeed a little afraid and moved at the same time. As I stood there at the gate nothing had happened in twenty and more years.[10]

At other times he was conscious of not belonging any more to the life of his home fields, not participating in the daily round of country tasks, his services no longer required by man or beast.

It is wonderful to be back in one's native fields but a little unsatisfactory when one is not part of the general activity. People are worried about and talking about certain things and you are out of it.

O it is wonderful to be involved in life and to be worried by it. . . .[11] It is terrible to live here as I do presently, in the midst of ripening and harvested fields and not to be involved.[12]

One of the things that makes my stay in these native fields unsatisfactory is the absence of any sort of livestock around the house. Some people say wrongly that love is in giving. Love is also in demanding. Cattle demand our attention and so do other domestic creatures and looking after them the country seems fully populated again.

Long ago of a Sunday evening I'd remember I'd have to be home to milk the kicking cow or to keep an eye on the sow that was about to farrow. Now as I stand on a distant cross-roads it comes into my mind again and again with a shock that my presence anywhere in the world in fact is unnecessary. In happiness there is bondage.[13]

Kavanagh carried on a constant dialogue with himself about his relationship with his home fields and the world of his youth. He was aware of the importance to every man, and especially perhaps to the writer, of the first twenty years.

Most of us live all our days in the stores piled up before we are twenty. Now that I analyse myself I realise that throughout everything I write there is this constantly recurring motif of the need to go back. Why do we always need to go back? What is it we want to return to? Freud says, the womb, and there is something in it too. . . .[14]

At the same time he realised that there was no going back. An inseparable part of that early life was its complete unconsciousness and unawareness. Once a man has eaten of the tree of knowledge he cannot return to innocence. He may regain innocence and reach again the place from which he started, but it will be by a winding route through the world of experience, not by a simple return. He realised, too, the difficulty of re-working early material and getting right the angle at which he once saw Dublin or his attitude to cruelty to animals. There was a danger of being false, melodramatic or sentimental. The past had to be connected with the present if it was not to be dead.

It is possible to evoke something but this means that we are evoking not out of our memories but out of our eternal selves. We are digging for that part of ourself which never changes. It is hard to get the cutting edge of sincerity right for this operation.[15]

When Kavanagh became a poet he inevitably removed himself from the home fields. Poetry is a mode of contemplation and the very nature of contemplation, which is detached and critical, separates the poet from the general activity of the fair and the farm. But the poet who has once been in the fair and on the farm will not forget the world he has known, even if he cannot return to it.

Kavanagh's involvement in country life has clearly conditioned his approach to nature and the countryside. He does not walk out as a spectator in search of the picturesque or the beautiful. He once said that 'the fields looked at me more than I looked at them'.[16] He admitted the countryman's lack of interest in the cultivation of flowers in an article on 'The Lillies of the Field' but pointed out that this did not mean indifference.

Although there may not have been any conscious horti-cultivation the flowers that bloomed in the springtime and in

71

the summer had a deep effect on all our lives. If we did not look much at them they looked at us and they influenced our minds.

A man might be doing a bit of quarrying or trimming briars as he walked in a plantation kneedeep in bluebells but they had touched him just the same. In the towns we need the cultivated flower and to cultivate an interest in flowers.[17]

He never believed in a romantic pursuit of beauty in nature. He felt that walking should always be done with some practical purpose in mind, not simply to admire the view. He reversed W. H. Davies's oft-quoted exhortation to us to stand and stare at the world around us.

Memorable beauty comes to us obliquely while we are going about our troubled business.

W. H. Davies wrote:—

What is this life if, full of care
We have no time to stand and stare?

But Davies was wrong:

What is this life if, *not* full of care,
We do not let the cart-tracks stare
Into our hearts with love's despair?

This pursuit of beauty is one of the defects of the tourist's point of view. The tourist is in a hurry; he demands quick returns of the picturesque and the obvious. But for all that it is possible even when we pursue beauty or happiness to come upon oblique references to it. The job is to recognise them in the hurry. Not everybody can have the fields and lanes stare at him as they stare at a man driving a cow to a fair.[18]

Kavanagh loved the familiar and the humble in nature. The dandelion and the nettle meant more to him than the tiger-lily or the hollyhock.

Amid the most picturesque mountain scenery I might only see the remains of a pit of wizened mangolds and in the Botanic Gardens my heart would delight in a fringe of nettles by a wall.[19]

I know of no writer who is more aware of the beauty of weeds. Perhaps the weeds looked at him first but he certainly looked back at them, not with the eye of a farmer but with the eye of a poet. Not all pastoral poets have loved, or even noticed, the weeds of the field. George Crabbe noticed them, but with disapproval, in *The Village*.

> Rank weeds, that every art and care defy,
> Reign o'er the land, and rob the blighted rye.

Kavanagh frankly abandons himself to the beauty and wonder of the weeds. He is speaking of himself when he writes of Tarry Flynn's response:

> The three big nettles that grew in the ring of boulders upon which last year's pikes of hay had stood were rich with the beauty of what is richly alive. The dust of last year's hay and straw was so lovely it could almost make him want to prostrate himself upon it. Stones, clay, grass, the sunlight coming through the privet hedge. Why did he love such common things?[20]

He loved them because they were a part of his being, and because he saw them with the vision of love and wonder, by the light of the poet's imagination. Although he moved away from farmyard and fair and felt himself separated from the life he was once a part of, he never forgot or renounced that early vision. When he is defining the poet's aim he still remembers the weeds. 'The purpose of the poet is to give people an enthusiasm for life, to draw their attention to the wonder of the fields, of the weeds.' [21]

The mode and the moods of the 'Monaghan' poems follow naturally from Kavanagh's general approach to his home fields. In most of them there is a relaxed, easy acceptance of the country world, without any straining or standing on tiptoe to catch a glimpse of wonder. 'Peace', written in Dublin in 1943, is an early but excellent example.

> And sometimes I am sorry when the grass
> Is growing over the stones in quiet hollows
> And the cocksfoot leans across the rutted cart-pass
> That I am not the voice of country fellows

Who now are standing by some headland talking
Of turnips and potatoes or young corn
Or turf banks stripped for victory.
Here Peace is still hawking
His coloured combs and scarves and beads of horn.

Upon a headland by a whinny hedge
A hare sits looking down a leaf-lapped furrow
There's an old plough upside-down on a weedy ridge
And someone is shouldering home a saddle-harrow.
Out of that childhood country what fools climb
To fight with tyrants Love and Life and Time.

The mode of this is neither Horatian nor Wordsworthian, but plain 'Monaghan'. Kavanagh remembers, not the primrose or the daffodil, but the cocksfoot and the grass growing over the stones. This is not the Ireland of wild mountain and glen, not the land-scape of Paul Henry or Seán Keating, but the quiet unexciting landscape of the little tillage fields. It is observed from the inside. The detail, deliberately commonplace, is sharply focussed and remembered with affection: 'an old plough upside-down on a weedy ridge'. The tone and movement of the verse is relaxed; the words seem casual and yet the lines fall with a quiet force in a firm pattern of rhyme, so that we accept the almost rhetorical lift of the last couplet. It is a much finer poem than the far more famous 'Lake Isle of Innisfree', in which Yeats is similarly explor-ing a vision of rural peace. Yeats's vision is romantic and senti-mental, and his nine bean rows belong to a fairy world rather than the world of country fellows.

Some of the 'Monaghan' poems reach far back into childhood. 'A Christmas Childhood', perhaps the most widely known and popular of all Kavanagh's poems, recalls the excitement of a six-year-old boy on Christmas morning.

One side of the potato-pits was white with frost —
How wonderful that was, how wonderful!
And when we put our ears to the paling-post
The music that came out was magical.

.   .   .   .

Outside in the cowhouse my mother
Made the music of milking;
The light of her stable-lamp was a star
And the frost of Bethlehem made it twinkle.

This poem makes a ready appeal to religious sentiment and this perhaps accounts for its great popularity in Ireland, but it is saved from sentimentality by sharply observed local detail. At the same time it has a musical grace and lightness of movement.

In other poems Kavanagh recalls the country tasks he once performed. 'Art McCooey' begins:

I recover now the time I drove
Cart-loads of dung to an outlying farm —

This seems a pedestrian beginning even for a poem of country reminiscence, but the poem as a whole succeeds in creating the Monaghan world and the gossip of two young men, with an affectionate intimacy that draws the reader into that world. The names of local people contribute to the effect of intimacy and reality.

Down the laneway of the popular banshees
By Paddy Bradley's; mud to the ankles;
A hare is grazing in Mat Rooney's meadow;
Maggie Byrne is prowling for dead branches.

The parish is part of the universe. In the last verse the mundane practical details merge into a wider perspective.

Wash out the cart with a bucket of water and a wangel
Of wheaten straw. Jupiter looks down.
Unlearnedly and unreasonably poetry is shaped
Awkwardly but alive in the unmeasured womb.

Kavanagh's country poems do not always come off. 'Primrose' is portentous and sentimental. It is in fact an earlier poem that seems to have strayed into *A Soul for Sale*. 'Spraying the Potatoes' for the most part catches beautifully the relaxed familiar tone that is characteristic of Kavanagh at his best:

And over that potato-field
A lazy veil of woven sun.
Dandelions growing on headlands, showing
Their unloved hearts to everyone.

but the image in the first verse of this poem is forced and pretentious:

Beside an orchard wall where roses
Were young girls hanging from the sky.

One of the simplest and yet most effective poems of Monaghan reminiscence is 'Kerr's Ass'. This was published in *Envoy* in October, 1950, and then appeared later in *Come Dance with Kitty Stobling*.

We borrowed the loan of Kerr's big ass
To go to Dundalk with butter,
Brought him home the evening before the market
An exile that night in Mucker.

We heeled up the cart before the door,
We took the harness inside —
The straw-stuffed straddle, the broken breeching
With bits of bull-wire tied:

The winkers that had no choke-band,
The collar and the reins. . . .
In Ealing Broadway, London Town
I name their several names

Until a world comes to life —
Morning, the silent bog,
And the God of imagination waking
In a Mucker fog.

The form and rhythm and language of this poem are almost childishly simple (though there is a subtle shift of rhythm in the last verse) and yet the world of Mucker, so strangely remote from Ealing Broadway, comes vividly through to the reader. The authentic detail of the humble harness creates an impression of complete fidelity to experience.

5

JOURNALIST AND CRITIC

Ladies and Gentlemen, I write from Dublin which is better than nowhere.[1]

The poems discussed in the last chapter were all written after Kavanagh had left Monaghan and settled in Dublin. His love-hate relationship with his environment was not confined to the country. He said many harsh things about Dublin, but he praised it and loved it too, and in later years he was to find a deep peace on the banks of the Grand Canal. Pembroke Road and Baggot Street became as important to him as Kednaminsha and Shancoduff.

The poet's position in the twentieth century, wherever he may live, is a complex and uncertain one. He has to make a living and he has to come to some sort of terms with the world he lives in. He has no natural niche, no accepted position in society. He may have to be teacher or civil servant first, and poet second. He may drift into a Bohemian underworld.

Kavanagh had no taste for the Bohemian underworld of Dublin, which shocked his sense of respectability, and he had few qualifications that could bring him work in the city. So he turned to journalism for a living and for the rest of his life he was to earn money by writing, both regularly and occasionally, for newspapers and magazines. He began in a humble way with articles in the *Irish Times* and a personal column for the *Irish Press* by 'Piers Plowman'. He also did book-reviewing and later on he became a film critic. Some of his journalism was simple hack-work, but much of it goes far beyond this. His lively and creative mind found a channel of expression in the most unlikely places. There are many striking and interesting passages in his book and film reviews, and by the early fifties, when he was writing a diary in *Envoy* and later producing *Kavanagh's Weekly,* he had developed a powerful and original voice as a journalist.

In one of his reviews he asks the question: 'What is the difference between literature and journalism?' and he supplies his own answer: 'Literature is written from the inside — journalism from the outside.'[2] But he himself was not the kind of man who could neatly divide his literature from his journalism. What gives life and interest to his newspaper columns, his book-reviewing and his film criticism, is the fact that he cannot write for long from the outside. His own *daimon* is too strong to be suppressed. His criticism is not detached and judicial, but impulsive and personal. He must write from the inside if he is to write at all.

He seldom gets down to systematic or detailed literary criticism, nor would we expect this in casual weekly reviewing. But he can strike out a bold, shrewd and vivid judgement that is worth pages from duller and more systematic critics. He says of Shaw, for example:

> The impact of the totality of his work is like a blow on the head from a paper bagful of peanuts rather than the terrible hammer blow delivered by a great poet or mystic — even a mystic of (in my opinion) evil, like Marx. Shaw is a great journalist, a man with tremendous energy and a semi-profound knowledge of many things. . . .[3]

Commenting on Hopkin's use of sprung rhythm he points out perceptively the nervous intensity of Hopkin's verse.

> In this nervous mould, it was, and is, impossible for a poet to spread out. It is a constricted form that forces thought deep down as into a narrow tunnel where the sharp rocks project from the sides. . . .[4]

Kavanagh's book reviewing shows a considerable increase of self-confidence when compared with his Piers Plowman column, and a much more controlled and incisive style. He continued this development in his criticism of films.

He leaves the reader in no doubt about his point of view. The popular Hollywood product appalled him. Most films were 'low, lewd and illiterate',[5] and very few could stir the imagination at all. He is even more scathing in his attack on the pretentious film that claimed to be taken seriously as Art. He had a deep distrust of Art and Culture, with capital letters. Indeed he raged against art in the head much as Lawrence raged against sex in the head. Theorising

78

about art and attempting to isolate art as an end in itself seemed to him merely pretentious posturing.

As a guide to films he is not altogether reliable. He is sometimes unfair and he occasionally talks nonsense, but he never simply follows a current intellectual fashion. It is always Kavanagh speaking his own mind. Who else would dismiss *Tom Jones* for being 'as painful as any piece of buckleppin' Irishry at the Abbey Theatre';[6] or point out that Disney films, though wonderfully inventive, 'lack the warmth of imagination'.[7]

Kavanagh's most sustained and vigorous critical writing and journalism appeared in the early fifties. From December 1949 to July 1951 he contributed to *Envoy* a lively and provocative diary. *Envoy* was a literary monthly published at 39 Grafton Street, Dublin, and edited by John Ryan, who was assisted by Valentin Iremonger and J. K. Hillman. It ran for twenty months and then died, chiefly for lack of funds. As usual Kavanagh's contributions cover a wide range of varied topics from the poetry of W. H. Auden to Gaelic football. He nearly always has something interesting and original to say; he is often prejudiced, sometimes cantankerous; he contradicts himself, but he is never vapid or dull.

His criticism and comment has been dismissed as merely chaotic and absurd. Hubert Butler remarked in an article in *The Bell*, another Dublin literary journal, that: 'Mr. Kavanagh's mind, when he abandons poetry and fiction, is like a monkey house at feeding time.'[8] This is no more than a picturesque exaggeration. Through *Envoy* and through *Kavanagh's Weekly* and other miscellaneous critical writings there runs a fairly consistent attitude to literature and to life, a Kavanagh way of feeling and thinking that is serious and challenging, a Kavanagh voice. In a public lecture delivered at Queen's University, Belfast, in 1964, he referred to it as 'my angry foghorn'. It may be loud and irritating, but it is not only the noise that compels us to listen.

Kavanagh's Weekly, a journal of literature and politics, appeared in the spring and summer of 1952. In appearance it was a humble newsheet. Each issue contained eight pages and it sold at the modest price of sixpence. It survived for thirteen issues, from 12 April to 5 July, at a loss of some eight hundred pounds. The loss is not surprising, since it had no advertisement revenue to speak of. It was a remarkable *tour de force* of journalism; nearly all the articles were written by Kavanagh himself under various pseudonyms. Almost his sole helper was his brother Peter, who wrote some of the articles and acted as publisher.

In the public lecture at the Queen's University mentioned above, Kavanagh referred to *Kavanagh's Weekly* as 'the best autobiography of the years when I was violent and funny'. The journal certainly is both violent and funny, though at times the violence outruns the humour. The first article in the first number is entitled 'Victory of Mediocrity' and it is a general onslaught on the Republic of Ireland.

> All the mouthpieces of public opinion are controlled by men whose only qualification is their inability to think.
> Being stupid and illiterate is the mark of respectability and responsibility. . . .
> The country is dead or dying of its false materialism.

The mirror that Kavanagh holds up to Ireland might remind us of the mirror that Yeats held up in his poem *September 1913*, with its chorus,

> Romantic Ireland's dead and gone.

But where Yeats deplores the absence of beautiful lofty things, the heroic gesture, 'all that delirium of the brave', Kavanagh deplores the lack of vitality, of intellectual excitement, of central passion.

> Nothing matters in the end but the imagination, the inner mind, the dream of hope that is in the heart of man . . . the great wet blanket of Fianna Fáil smothers the imaginative life of this country.

In both *Envoy* and *Kavanagh's Weekly* he saw the main function of criticism as the destruction of the false.

> All healthy criticism is destructive. What is needed is not so much fostering of the best as preventing what little best there is being submerged in the general flattery of the mediocre.[9]
> A true creative critic is a sweeping critic who violently hates certain things because they are weeds which choke the field against the crop which he wants to sow. Truth is personality and no genuine writer as a critic was ever anything but absolute in his destructiveness.[10]

Kavanagh's viewpoint is essentially that of the creative writer with personal convictions of his own. Much of his criticism is clearing the field to make room for his own utterance. This helps to explain his sharp attack on the writers of the Irish literary movement associated with the Abbey Theatre. He abuses Synge and even Yeats because he felt that their example and influence were a danger to real creative vitality and originality in his time.

> The mentality which was Yeats's enemy is everywhere in power, and that mentality thrives by praising Yeats. The adulation of Yeats and of Joyce has become a menace to the living, for when a dead poet is praised, something is praised that isn't the real thing at all. Death changes the whole position, so that to be on the side of truth one would need to damn dead poets. Death is static, while the living change, and sometimes without realising it, men imagine that they are on the same side as they were when the poet was alive.[11]

Kavanagh is overstating his case, or as he has put it himself, he is 'sharpening the edge of truth to make it sink in'.[12] It would clearly be absurd if we had to damn all dead poets. And yet there may well be a need for present poets and thinkers to damn, or at least to resist the influence of, the previous generation, the recently dead.

Kavanagh denounced Synge not only because he felt him to be a bad example to younger writers, encouraging a phoney 'Irishness', a folksy, false approach to tinkers and peasants, but also because he felt his work was superficial, a portrayal of peasant life from the outside.

> His peasants are picturesque conventions; the language he invented for them did a disservice to letters in this country by drawing our attention away from the common speech whose delightfulness comes from its very ordinariness. One phrase of Joyce is worth all Synge as far as giving us the cadence of Irish speech. . . .
>
> Synge provided Irish Protestants who are worried about being "Irish" with an artificial country. . . .[13]

Kavanagh is unfair to Synge because he was engaged in a bitter battle with 'the Irish thing', which threatened to engulf him in his younger days, and which he felt was a constant danger to contemporary writers in Ireland. The temptation to manufacture a bogus 'Irish' article that would appeal to English and American readers was a real threat, though it did perhaps assume unreally monstrous proportions in Kavanagh's eyes.

In his passionate struggle against the ghosts of the Abbey Theatre he takes the side of those who rioted against *The Playboy of the Western World*, accuses Synge of hate and coarseness and vulgar superficiality. But in calmer moments he does admit that Synge has the creative intoxication of the spirit that is the basis of genius. Taken as fantasy, not as a true picture of Irish life, *The Playboy* is enjoyable. 'The gaiety of *The Playboy* is not dependent on its Western background. Synge was a minor poet but an authentic one. . . .' [1a]

Synge, of course, never claimed to be a realist. He only defended the reality of the dialogue and incidents in his plays from the charge that they were utterly untrue to Irish experience. Synge was defending himself against fanatical Nationalists. It is ironic that this later violent onslaught on his reputation should come from one of the bitterest opponents of Nationalism that twentieth century Ireland has yet produced.

Kavanagh's quarrel with Yeats is less easy to define than his quarrel with Synge. It is partly that he finds the man hidden behind a mask.

You never fall in love with anything in Yeats because his private world does not enlarge into a world for everyman. He does not evoke pity, passion or anger, and for all his burden of his native country in his work no poet could be more outside what we may call the Irish consciousness, and this is because he is too detached, too careful, too prudent to be human. He wrote ballads which he foolishly hoped would be popular with the people, but the people sensed this artificial note. Yeats wrote at a consistently high level but one single scream of the heart that pierces heavens he could never reach. For this reason he leaves me cold and leaves me in much doubt about his ultimate survival. Yeats belongs not to Sligo or to Ireland but was a child of the Victorian myth. He was the last Eminent Victorian. Yet it is impossible for us to read some of his later

82

poems without bowing to the magical technique, and feeling that he is at last dining with Landor and Donne.[15]

In calling Yeats 'the last Eminent Victorian' he has deftly summed up one aspect of Yeats's personality and rhetoric; but he sharpens the edge of truth too keenly when he discounts his relationship with Sligo or Ireland. In a later article, his contribution to the centenary comment on Yeats in the *Irish Times*, he allowed Yeats his Irishness.

His attitude to Yeats is curiously ambivalent and equivocal. He damns in one sentence and praises in another. He acknowledged that Yeats was a great poet and 'more than a great poet, he was a great man. . . . It is the pressure of a fine mind that gives to many of his slight poems their impact.'[16] But he could never quite warm to Yeats. And he felt that Yeats, like other writers of the movement that he created, had helped to foster the dangerous and baleful myth that Ireland was a spiritual entity.

The Irish writers to whom he gave the greatest praise were William Carleton and James Joyce. He made many approving references to Carleton and wrote about him at some length. He particularly admired his *Traits and Stories of the Irish Peasantry*. He wrote a feature article for the *Irish Times* bookpage in 1945.

> If ever there was a writer of the people as well as a writer for the people William Carleton was such a one. In a great many small farmers' houses when I was growing up in the North you would be liable to find one of Duffy's prayer-book-like editions of this novelist sharing library honours in the back window with old Moore's Almanac.[17]

He praises Carleton for giving us authentic pictures of peasant life, in tones and turns of speech that are vivid and accurate, for interpreting for us material facts 'in terms of that joy which is also part of Reality'.[18]

In July 1951 he gave a talk on the B.B.C. Third Programme on 'Carleton and Irishness'. He dismisses Synge as not being authentically Irish and cites with approval a remark by Yeats that Carleton was the 'greatest Irish writer'. Although Carleton sometimes tried to offer the English public a stereotyped Paddy, when he wrote at his best he portrayed, from the inside, the common life that he knew. 'His best contribution to posterity is that he preserved for it a people and a culture before its continuity was destroyed by the Great Famine.'[19] Kavanagh illustrates Carleton's vivid and authentic speech, and his comic detachment as a story-teller, by quoting passages from the *Traits and Stories*.

He wrote of Carleton again in the *Irish Farmers' Journal* in June 1962, shortly after a selection of Carleton's stories, edited by Anthony Cronin, had been published. Here he denies that the continuity with Carleton's world had been entirely destroyed.

> The editor of the present edition says that the life that Carleton depicts disappeared entirely with the Famine etc., but this is not true. The very same life and the very same way of speech lived on into my day.
>
> There is the account of Shane Fadh's wedding and my father and many others I know attended precisely the same sort of wedding with the running for the bottle and the lot of it.[20]

When we listen to the voice of Mrs. Flynn in *Tarry Flynn* I think we can recognise that her world is not so far removed from that of Nancy McKeown in the *Traits and Stories*.

It was Kavanagh's opinion that Joyce had done more for Ireland than Yeats. Through *Ulysses* the City of Dublin had entered the world of literature. In an article on Dublin in the *Encyclopedia Americana* (1957) he wrote:

> In 1904 Yeats opened the Abbey theatre and the city was fully alive again. But the most important thing that was happening in Dublin at this time was not the activity of Yeats and his followers but the fact that wandering in the city, unknown and ignored, was a young man whose observant eye and ear was capturing the epic city that is to be found in *Ulysses*. As Cyril Connolly says, "What Baudelaire and Laforgue did for Paris, or T. S. Eliot for modern London, Joyce did for Dublin." As an evocation of a city, as the truth that never gets into the history books, it would be impossible to over-estimate the importance of *Ulysses*.

Ulysses was Kavanagh's second-favourite bedside book, but he regarded Joyce less as a creative genius than as a 'very clever cynical man who has found a formula'. '*Ulysses*,' he writes, 'is a very funny book and it is also a very wearying book. It is almost entirely a transcription of life.' [21] Elsewhere he qualifies this by saying that the book 'is only incidentally about Dublin and fundamentally the history of a soul'.[22]

Ulysses is the only Irish book that Kavanagh lists among the books that most deeply interested him. The others were *Moby Dick*, *Gil Blas* and Knut Hamsun's *The Wanderers*. This seems a strange list, but Kavanagh found in them the spiritual food that he needed. He remarks in passing: 'I happen not to be very interested in books.' [23] He certainly did not read to get a knowledge of 'literature' or to keep up with literary fashion. He read only what interested him at the moment, and the books he liked he read and re-read. He read *Moby Dick* many times. It seemed to be written 'out of the blind life', to go below the surface into the life of the unconscious. 'It enlarges the world for us; it brings us through the ivory gates into the expansive world of the imagination.' [24]

He admitted that *Gil Blas* was only light entertainment, but it fascinated him. 'There is really nothing to it — incident piled on incident — and yet we are intoxicated. I have read *Gil Blas* at least a hundred times. I am a bad example for book buyers.' [25]

Wanderers only just gets a place on his short list of three or four books, but he often referred to it with love and reverence. '*Wanderers* is a pure poem as wonderful as *Moby Dick*. I have read it at least fifty times and can quote some of its phrases from memory.' [26]

Perhaps it is not without significance that the central figures in all four of these books are wanderers — wanderers in search of love, of life, and of something intangible to quench the thirst of the mortal soul.

Kavanagh is not a reliable guide to books and writers any more than he is to films. He is a hit-and-miss critic, but when he does hit he frequently scores a telling bull's eye, and at least he always shoots his own arrows. Although his criticism is not sustained or methodical, and it has something of a take-it-or-leave-it air, he sometimes goes to the heart of the matter in one sentence or phrase. His brief assessment of Irish writers in an *Envoy* article is worth a book by a more methodical and less perceptive critic. For example here are his short comments on Padraic Colum, James Stephens and Æ.

Colum's early impulse was original. His poems and some of his ballads evoke a valid mood. *The Poor Scholar of the Forties* is a fine poem. His *Plougher*, with its

> Sunset, a man, around him earth savage, earth broken

is Whitman at his worst, thinking that by shouting you can get the ear of God.

James Stephens as a story-teller has genius, but much of his verse is unalive, barren, whimsy:

> Left and right and swing around
> Soar and dip and fall for glee,
> Happy sky and bird and ground.
> Happy wind, and happy tree. . . .

Æ, a remarkable man, wrote some good poems, and it was a pity that he should have buried his authentic genius in the vasty deeps of the Upanishads.[27]

There are some major writers with whom Kavanagh had no sympathy, and his comments on them tend to be simply derogatory and unilluminating. He dismisses Ibsen as a 'phoney and a heretic'. Of D. H. Lawrence he remarked: 'I tried to read his novels. He's impossible. He's pathetic and preposterous.'[28] One is sharply reminded of Lawrence's own comments on some of the writers he disliked. A man who dislikes Lawrence might be expected to like Jane Austen, but she is equally distasteful to Kavanagh. He lumps her with Elizabeth Bowen and other women writers as superficial, unable to reach beyond mortal walls into the world of the imagination.

> Jane Austen or Elizabeth Bowen or any woman writer one can name deals with the material ramifications of human nature. You can think of this kind of writing as brilliant only when you have lost faith in the Imagination.[29]
> . . . Jane Austen whose delayed-action tricks give such an illusion of cunning, subtlety and delicious wit, and whose brilliant handling of what isn't worth handling has such an appeal for the middle-classes who delight in brilliant technique with the minimum of reality.[30]

86

He was hardly more responsive to the novels of Dickens. He found them 'dull, sentimental and utterly unreal . . . let me truthfully say that I have never been able to read a Dickens novel'.[31] But later on he softened towards Dickens, and he does put him among the great English writers.

Kavanagh's best criticism is often called forth by specific examples of writing in front of him. When he is looking at a piece of verse or prose in front of him he is more perceptive than when he is making sweeping generalisations about writers he dislikes — or even those he likes. False coin, in verse or prose, did not easily escape his keen glance. In reviewing a book by Joseph O'Connor, entitled *Hostage to Fortune,* he picks out the following sentences.

> "It was August 1894. The long summer holidays were drawing to an end in a swelter of sunshine and I was as happy as a pup with two tails."
>
> Most readers would say that the simile, "a pup with two tails" is original and very expressive, yet it kills the writing, for it is insincere; it is not felt, it is merely a clever phrase. If he had said "I was happy and don't know why" he might have won our affection, or he might have evoked it by some small event. But then that is experience.[32]

On another occasion a poem by Edith Sitwell caught his eye.

> It was the time when the vulture left my heart in cold
>   December. . . .
> And I did not know which was my heart and which the
>   rook. . . .
> But I remember
> The echo of my breath in the street's wintry weather.

I read with a feeling of sadness this poem in *The Listener* by Edith Sitwell. There is a good example of a woman making what we'd call 'a cod of herself'. She has deluded herself that she is a prophetic poet and the result is something ludicrous. It is a bubble in which she lives and if it burst she would be a very pathetic person. . . .

> It was the time when the vulture left my heart. . . .

What does that mean?

It is the language of mysticism and of experience without either mysticism or experience.[33]

Kavanagh's likes and dislikes are often arbitrary and passionate. His angry foghorn might startle and annoy the reader, but he would be likely to read on. The *Envoy* diaries and the articles in *Kavanagh's Weekly* were never safe and dull, nor were they smart and empty.

The penultimate number of *Kavanagh's Weekly* carried the following notice prominently displayed in a box on the front page.

> The next issue of this paper will be the final one; it will be a limited edition, autographed by the Editor, and it will be sold only as part of the complete file. The price of the complete file will be £1 and it will be available only from
>
> ### P. KAVANAGH
> 62 Pembroke Road, Dublin.
>
> If, however, we receive in the meantime a sum of £1,000 or upwards we will distribute next week's issue in the ordinary way and continue publishing KAVANAGH'S WEEKLY.

No daring patron came forward with £1,000. The paper ended with the next issue, number 13. Only a handful of people contributed even the £1 asked for, and Kavanagh burnt a pile of unwanted copies. The head barman of McDaid's pub in Dublin remarked to a reporter: 'Paddy said the biggest black mark he ever saw was the black mark against the wall of his flat when he burnt the unsold copies of *Kavanagh's Weekly*.'[34]

A complete set of these little sixpenny magazines is now a rare and expensive bookseller's item.

6

ON THE BANKS OF THE GRAND CANAL

In his characteristic sweeping way Kavanagh swept aside nearly all the poetry he had written up to 1955, including *The Great Hunger* and *A Soul for Sale*. In his *Self-Portrait* he remarks:

> For many a good-looking year I wrought hard at versing but I would say that, as a poet, I was born in or about nineteen-fifty-five, the place of my birth being the banks of the Grand Canal.[1]

The early fifties were troubled times for Kavanagh. His literary reputation was established and he had become one of the most publicised and most controversial literary figures in Dublin. Not long after the closing down of *Kavanagh's Weekly* a 'Profile' of him appeared in the *Leader,* an Irish weekly. The anonymous author praised his poetry but gave a personal picture of him that he deeply resented. It presented him as a clown and 'character', a mixture of inspired idiot and rollicking bar-room prophet, surrounded by admiring young beatniky disciples whom he despised. This is how the profile begins:

> "A pard-like spirit, beautiful and swift", is hardly the phrase that would occur to the mind of the casual observer watching Mr. Kavanagh hunkering on a bar-stool, defining alcohol as the worst enemy of the Imagination. The great voice, reminiscent of a load of gravel sliding down the side of a quarry, booms out, the starry-eyed young poets and painters surrounding him — all of them twenty or more years his junior, convinced (rightly, too) that the Left Bank was never like this — fervently cross themselves, there is a slackening, noticeable enough in the setting-up of the balls of malt. With a malevolent insult which, naturally, is well received, the Master orders a further measure, and, cocking an eye at the pub-clock, downs the malt in a gulp which produces a fit of coughing that all but stops even the traffic outside. His acolytes — sylph-like

redheads, dewy-eyed brunettes, two hard-faced intellectual blondes, three rangy university poets and several semi-bearded painters — flap: "Yous have no merit, no merit at all" — he insults them individually and collectively, they love it, he suddenly leaves to get lunch in the Bailey and have something to win on the second favourite. He'll be back.[2]

Kavanagh felt that the article damaged his position as a serious writer and he sued the *Leader* for libel. The case came before the court in February 1954, and it was something of a *cause célèbre* in Dublin. Kavanagh had to stand up to long hours of cross-examination in the witness-box. The hearing lasted seven days, and judgement was finally given against him. Looking back on it many years later he was able to see it as comedy, but at the time it must have seriously affected his health and his spirits.

Early in 1955 he entered the old Rialto Hospital for an operation. He had contracted lung cancer and one of his lungs was removed. He recovered and was able to walk out and convalesce on the banks of the Grand Canal. He later referred to his two months in the Rialto hospital as the happiest time of his life.

> Shortly after I left, the Rialto changed hands, was closed and later became part of St. Kevin's. Often I would wander around that area looking longingly at that concrete building where part of my life lay buried, and sad that I could not go in, talk to the girl at the desk, go up the stairs, pass along the rows of cubicles in the non T.B. sector and live again the happiest hours of my life.[3]

He wrote a sonnet, 'The Hospital', and he gave a Radio talk, 'My Hospital Notebook', on his impressions of hospital. It was clearly an important experience for him. The regular routine, the friendliness of the nurses, the attention of visitors, gave him a sense of security and repose. 'Probably the real attraction of a hospital,' he wrote later, 'as well as of prisons and monasteries is the discipline.'[4]

But it was the convalescence, the rebirth into the world of sunshine and grass and water, that gave rise to a new mood and a new outpouring of poetry, a resurgence of the feeling of love and wonder that he had felt in earlier days in Monaghan.

My hegira was to the Grand Canal Bank where again I saw the beauty of water and green grass and the magic of light. It was the same emotion as I had known when I stood on a sharp slope in Monaghan where I imaginatively stand now, looking across to Slieve Gullion and South Armagh.[5]

The new mood finds expression in the two canal bank sonnets and in other poems later collected in the volume *Come Dance with Kitty Stobling*. Kavanagh remarked in an accompanying note, that he wrote these poems 'in an orgy of energy in about a week'.[6] It was certainly a flowering time for his spirit and his pen. His angry foghorn was forgotten and a flowing joy and peace accompanies his acceptance of the unworn world. He discovers again that 'God is in the bits and pieces of everyday'. The relaxed yet joyful note is struck in the opening of the first sonnet, 'Canal Bank Walk'.

Leafy-with-love banks and the green waters of the canal,
Pouring redemption for me, that I do
The will of God, wallow in the habitual, the banal,
Grow with nature again as before I grew.

The Grand Canal, which links Dublin to towns in the west of Ireland, encircles a part of the town before joining the Liffey. It forms something of a thin green belt between the city and the suburbs. Kavanagh's favourite haunt was between the bridges at Baggot Street and Leeson Street. It is shown in the background to the photograph of Kavanagh on the sleeve of his gramophone record, 'Almost Everything'. On the bank, near a lock, two seats were erected 'to the Memory of Mrs. Dermot O'Brien'.* Here Kavanagh sat 'in the tremendous silence of mid-July' and found his way to 'Parnassian islands'. To a passing tourist there will seem nothing very much to inspire poetry in this stretch of urban canal. The water is rather shallow and often disfigured with the rubbish of the town. But, as Kavanagh says in his lines on the hospital:

Nothing whatever is by love debarred
The common and banal her heat can know

---

*Another seat, on the south side of the Canal, was erected in memory of Patrick Kavanagh, in 1968.

The secret of his new vision of the common world is an outflowing of love and praise.

> I want to throw myself on the public street without caring
> For anything but the prayering that the earth offers.

There is a feeling of joyful surprise, expressed explicitly in 'Song at Fifty', that 'an unthrifty Man turned of Fifty' without wife or child is aware of spiritual possessions, of the grace of poetry.

> An undisciplined person
> Through futile excitements arsing
> Finds in his spendthrift purse
> A bankbook writ in verse
> And borrowers of purity
> Offering substantial security
> To him who just strayed
> Through a lifetime without a trade.

The glow of love and gratitude gives to the poems of this period a warmth and ease, an outflowing of joy that is felt in the rhythm of the verse. They are Kavanagh's happiest poems. The glow is perhaps strongest in the sonnets, the two on the canal bank, the 'three coloured sonnets', 'October' and 'Kitty Stobling'. But the energy of happiness is in all the poems. It is in the ballad about himself, 'If Ever You Go to Dublin Town'. Kavanagh frequently sang this ballad, which goes to a popular ballad tune. It ends with the lines

> Yet he lived happily
> I tell you.

He sang this ballad at the Guinness lecture he gave at the Queen's University in 1964. At the end he said: 'I'm afraid after twenty years I don't agree with the last line.' He was then in one of his gloomier moods. After singing the ballad on his record he simply comments quizzically: 'I wonder?'

One important aspect of his 'hegira' is the rejection of an old self, 'the sticky self that clings', and the re-discovery of a new self that has the freedom of Parnassus. The 'sticky self' is over-earnest, angry and self-pitying. In 'The Self-Slaved' he decides to throw it away

With its self-righteous
Satirising blotches.

In the second part of 'Auditors In' he finds a different Self.

I turn away to where the Self reposes
The placeless Heaven that's under all our noses
Where we're shut off from all the barren anger
No time for self-pitying melodrama . . .
    . . . I am so glad.
To come so accidently upon
My Self at the end of a tortuous road.

'To let experience enter the soul. Not to be self-righteous. . . . I discovered that the important thing above all was to avoid taking oneself sickly seriously', he wrote in his autobiographical note, 'From Monaghan to the Grand Canal'.[7] And he remarked in *Self-Portrait* that he learnt the secret of 'how not to care'. This 'no caring jag' is not, of course, apathy or indifference. It is miles away in spirit from the wish to escape involvement expressed in the popular phrase 'I couldn't care less'. 'Not caring is really a sense of values and feeling of confidence.'[8] It is the poet's serenity and detachment, an avoidance of anger, self-righteousness, earnestness and didacticism.

The important thing is not
To imagine one ought
Have something to say,
A raison d'être, a plot for the play.
The only true teaching
Subsists in watching. . . .
To look on is enough
In the business of love.

The poet's freedom from 'ponderosity' is expressed in the casual movement of the verse. The style of 'Is' and many of the short-lined poems in *Come Dance with Kitty Stobling* is very different from some of his earlier work.

One of the most successful poems in this new mode is 'To Hell with Commonsense'. The theme, the rejection of reason and commonsense, runs through the poems of this period. It is one aspect of the acceptance of love's mystery.

> More kicks than pence
> We get from commonsense
> Above its door is writ
> All hope abandon. It
> Is a bank will refuse a post
> Dated cheque of the Holy Ghost.
> Therefore I say to hell
> With all reasonable
> Poems in particular
> We want no secular
> Wisdom plodded together
> By concerned fools.

There is an energy and gaiety in this that gives life to the casual near-doggerel movement. The image of 'the post-dated cheque of the Holy Ghost' is striking and original, and expresses exactly the poet's scorn for the plodding prudence of secular wisdom that rejects the only thing really worth having. The poem combines seriousness with levity. It re-states in wholly contemporary terms the paradox of the gospels: 'He that saveth his soul shall lose it.'

The manner of this poem, and of several others such as 'Is' and 'Song at Fifty', is entirely different from that of the canal-bank sonnets and 'October'. Kavanagh's re-birth by the Grand Canal had given him a new range and freedom, 'To walk Parnassus right into the sunset'.

7

DR. JOHNSON AT McDAID'S*

It will by now be very clear to the reader that Kavanagh is a writer with a strong personality that colours all he writes. Although he wrote in a wide variety of styles and forms, his subject is basically the same — himself.

This does not mean that his range is narrow and egocentric; but he is in the ranks of the confessional writers, with St. Augustine, Rousseau, Wordsworth and D. H. Lawrence, rather than with those who portray a broad canvas of the human scene, such as Shakespeare, Balzac, Dickens and Browning. This division is of course a very crude one, but I hope it will serve to make my point.

As we read Kavanagh we are compulsively drawn into the orbit of his personality, and any attempt to assess his quality and position as a writer must sooner or later, come to grips with his strong but bewildering character. This is by no means easy. Kavanagh resists being gripped, by friend or foe; he is almost as slippery as the old man of the sea. A Dublin reviewer discussing *Self-Portrait* when it first appeared, called him

> a bundle of contradictions, publicity-seeker and hider-be-hind-smoke-screens, exponent and denouncer of "peasant-quality", at once arrogant about and contemptuous of his own work, capable of magic and capable of rubbish.[1]

The bewildering contradictoriness of Kavanagh's personality was reflected in the effect he had on other people. Some adored him, others found him impossible. Martin Green, an admirer, writes:

> I never met a man who loved
> Life so, or met the day so gay;
> Or whose person ever moved
> More blithely through this world or way.
>
> To meet you in a pub at noon
> Would guarantee a day well met;
> A heart as large as harvest moon
> And rich as any sun that set.[2]

---

*McDaid's Bar in Harry Street, Dublin, was a favourite haunt of Kavanagh's.

Donald Torchiana, discussing contemporary Irish poetry in *The Chicago Review* introduced Kavanagh as follows:

> To turn to Patrick Kavanagh is to turn to outrage. He shouldn't really exist. If Behan is a professional juvenile delinquent, then Kavanagh is even worse — a professional peasant. His bellowing and haranguing in newspapers, little mags, and lectures, like his appearance, is simply atrocious.[3]

In fairness to Torchiana, I should add that he went on to give high praise to some of Kavanagh's poetry.

Some commentators have sought to explain Kavanagh's enigmatic character by seeing a huge chip on his shoulder. John Hewitt called him a 'professional protester' and remarked that 'as an Angry Young Man, he preceded Mr. Osborne by a quarter of a century'.[4] This is too simple a judgement, but Kavanagh himself confessed to 'a fantastic inferiority complex'. It seems that his family and his neighbours did little to build up his self-confidence. I have already referred to his slowness in coming awake, becoming aware of himself and his potentialities.

> We learn too late that we are at least not unattractive. In fact we may be quite exciting. I am afraid I cannot compliment those that reared me for their wisdom in the matters. It was all so brutal. "You ugly-looking thing, you. Big-nose, humpy." All of this I am convinced springs from bad land . . . courage, gaiety, wisdom and so forth derive from the right kind of soil.[5]

One is hand-reminded of Christy Mahon in *The Playboy* who expected only contempt and abuse and was so astonished at sympathy and praise that he blossomed into a poet and a lover. There is a thinly disguised autobiographical piece in *Collected Pruse* called 'The Lay of the Crooked Knight' where Kavanagh describes himself. 'He was six feet tall, but angular, of graceless movement and eccentric mien.'[6] He is astonished to be chosen as a lover by a beautiful and wealthy lady.

> She *did* choose him, not *he* her, for he had a faint heart, due chiefly to his having it dinned into his head by his relations during his whole boyhood that he was the ugliest thing and the stupidest thing within the four walls of the country. To

96

make his chances worse he dressed badly, worse than badly —
execrably. Some days he was too lazy to shave or comb his
hair or put on a clean shirt or polish his shoes or have the hole
in the heel of his sock darned.[7]

After the lady has had some success in reforming the crooked
knight and making a smooth and successful citizen of him, she
leaves him for an active young country solicitor. He reacts by a
gesture of angry defiance in a polite city café.

> And then he rose from the table, gave one huge roar. He
> cursed everything and everybody. He spat on the floor. The
> crowd stared at him.[8]

After this the knight returns quickly to his crooked angularity.

One of Kavanagh's columns in the *Irish Farmers' Journal* is
headed, 'I was Not in the Swim'. He began: 'I have all my life
been cut off from what are probably the three greatest social
openings — I never learnt to dance, to swim or to drive a car. . . .'[9]

Perhaps he overestimates the social advantages of being able to
swim, but behind his words there is clearly a feeling of being
socially an outsider. He suggests that the reason he never learnt to
dance was simply conceit: 'I was afraid of being laughed at.'[10]

The same kind of difference and hesitation prevented him from
becoming an actor. For a time he attended the Abbey School of
Acting under Frank Dermody.

> Frank told me that I had a real future as an actor. But at
> that time I was very near thirty and all the others were under
> 25 so I felt embarrassed and left. It was a mistake, for, although
> acting on its own is rather a disappointing profession, tied up
> with some ability in a literary direction it could be a great
> advantage, Shakespeare himself was a bit of an actor.[11]

Kavanagh's early bent towards poetry increased his sense of
being an outsider. A poet was something of an oddity; indeed he
was close to an idiot. As an idiot he might be more amusing than
a poet. He remarks in *The Green Fool*:

> The people didn't want a poet, but a fool, yes they could be
> doing with one of these. And as I grew up not exactly 'like
> another' I was installed the fool.

I was the butt of many an assembly. . . . At wake, fair or dance for many years I was the fellow whom the jokers took a hand at when conversational funds fell low.[12]

We must not forget that *The Green Fool* is fictional autobiography rather than an exact recording from life; but the tone of this passage has the ring of reality and it suggests a further reason for Kavanagh's sense of being outside the common fold.

Although in later years he had many devoted friends, the image reflected from his writings is mainly a solitary one. The Green Fool, Tarry Flynn, the poet who conducts dialogues with himself in the *Envoy* diaries, the editor of *Kavanagh's Weekly,* all are somewhat lonely figures. Kavanagh was never one of an easy group of equals. Auden, Spender, Day Lewis, Rex Warner, all rubbed shoulders and minds together at Oxford. Had Kavanagh had similar opportunities of easy mixing in undergraduate society one wonders what the effect would have been. Would he have felt less hostility to the world of letters? Would he ever have become a writer at all?

In spite of the fact that he left school at the age of thirteen or so, he did not feel deprived of education. He picked up a great deal from reading and conversation. He had the kind of mind that could find the intellectual and spiritual food that it needed.

I may say that I have never been to school, but I have never felt that I was in any way hindered from what was mine to do, or saying my say; and I have never felt as some people say un-universitied men of genius feel, any discomfort or inferiority complex because of it.[13]

His feeling of inferiority, when he had it, was certainly not intellectual or cultural inferiority. He was indeed authoritarian and arrogant in his attitude, though arrogance can, of course, spring from a fear of inferiority.

I think Kavanagh's early years gave him an ingrained suspicion that people might treat him as a fool or a clown. This helps to explain his fierce attack on the image of the poet as an inspired idiot or a clown. At the same time he had a gift for clowning and he liked to entertain an audience. The contradictory impulses may account for a good deal in his writing and his life.

Whatever feeling of inferiority he may have had to struggle with,

98

Kavanagh certainly spoke with the voice of authority. He would dominate any discussion group in which he took part. Sometimes I am reminded of Dr. Johnson,* of whom Goldsmith once remarked: 'There is no arguing with Johnson; for when his pistol misses fire, he knocks you down with the butt-end of it.' [14] At first sight it might seem that Samuel Johnson and Patrick Kavanagh were poles apart, but on closer inspection we find that they have some remarkable similarities — so remarkable that I want to examine them in some detail.

Like Johnson, Kavanagh had a powerful and often disconcerting physical presence. Boswell tells us that Johnson's figure was 'large and well-formed and his countenance of the cast of an ancient statue'.[15] The Bellman, in a personal account of Kavanagh, remarks:

> Mr. Kavanagh — both mentally and physically as well as vocally — is constructed on what the sculptors call the 'heroic' scale, which is to say, rather a little larger than life. Rodin would have adored him as a model.[16]

Johnson was given to convulsive starts and odd gesticulations. There was an element of uncertainty about his behaviour in public. He would amaze a drawing-room by suddenly ejaculating a clause of the Lord's prayer. Once, in a moment of indignation, he threw a cup of tea out of a window. The Bellman, taking tea with Kavanagh in a café is conscious of 'what women novelists used to call 'the Elemental'.

> A great root-like hand shoots across the table to the toast dish, casting a thunder-cloud shadow on the cloth. P.K., without warning, suddenly crosses his legs, jerks the table a good two feet in the air, cups and dishes a jingle-jangling, and continues the conversation as if no earthquake had occurred. Or

---

*After I had written this chapter I found my impression confirmed by David Wright, who wrote: 'Dr. Johnson's subjugation of London seems the nearest parallel to Kavanagh's conquest of Dublin; an analogue not so far fetched as it might seem. Both were pub-men, both of formidable physical presence accentuated by a touch of the uncouth and by characteristic mannerisms; both devastating in argument. . . .' (*The London Magazine*, April, 1968.)

he as suddenly hunches the enormous, mountainous shoulders, and chairs, table, walls even, seem to shiver with him.[17]

Johnson often attracted attention as he walked along the streets of London by his strange gait and unusual movements. Kavanagh tells us that he may be noticed when walking along a Dublin street 'making wild vicious kicks at emptiness and scringing my teeth at the same time'.[18]

Both Johnson and Kavanagh were the victims of a compulsive neurosis, though Kavanagh seems only to have suffered from this in boyhood, whereas Johnson's neurosis was observed by Boswell in his later years. Boswell records that Johnson had an

> anxious care to go out or in at a door or passage by a certain number of steps from a certain point, or at least so that either his right or his left foot (I am not certain which) should constantly make the first actual movement when he came close to the door or passage.[19]

Boswell frequently found Johnson counting his steps or observed him going back to get his steps right. Kavanagh, in his youth, when crossing a road or railway line (there was a railway line between his home and the main road) felt compelled to leave road or line with his right foot last.

> People often saw me with one foot out behind me on the end of the sleeper; I was making sure that I did the job right and I was very nearly run over by trains on occasions.[20]

The physical similarities between Johnson and Kavanagh are interesting, but more important are the similarities of mind and attitude. Both men hated humbug and cant of any kind and expressed their hatred forcefully.

> My dear friend (Johnson said to Boswell), clear your *mind* of cant. You may talk as other people do; you may say to a man, "Sir, I am your humble servant". You are *not* his most humble servant. You may say, "These are bad times; it is a melancholy thing to be reserved to such times." You don't mind the times. You may *talk* in this manner; it is a mode of talking in society; but don't *think* foolishly.[21]

100

Johnson was indignant at the spurious and easy protestations of patriotism that were common in his day. This explains his famous definition of patriotism as 'the last refuge of a scoundrel', and his dry comment; 'when a butcher tells you that *his heart bleeds for his country* he has in fact, no uneasy feeling.'[22] Kavanagh's indignation was quickly aroused by anything that seemed phoney, especially anything 'Irish'. He, too, is sceptical about patriotism. He disliked the grandiloquent phrase, 'War of Independence', which was commonly used to describe the nationalist struggle in Ireland between 1916 and 1921.

There is something embarrassingly ostentatious about the term "War of Independence" as applied to what in more amusing days was called "the Troubles". Only a large country like the United States can carry the burden of such a term and it should be left to the United States.[23]

Anything that suggested intellectual cant or fashionable humbug drew Kavanagh's fire. He detested any talk of Art with a capital 'A', and any kind of literary jargon. In a literary discussion on the radio, one of the speakers mentioned 'the breaking down of semantic blocks' and 'the search for identity'. Kavanagh immediately rejected these phrases as meaningless: 'It is the greatest rubbish and jargon I ever heard in my life.'[24]

Both Johnson and Kavanagh helped to let a good deal of fresh air into the discussions and debates of their time, but of course they were both sometimes obstinately wrongheaded in condemning as humbug what they disliked; the pastoral convention of *Lycidas*, for example, or the peasant world of Synge.

In several other ways the strong personalities of Johnson and Kavanagh coincide. Both had a hearty contempt for and dislike of actors and the acting profession. Both were insensitive to music and had little success in learning to play a musical instrument. Johnson confessed to Boswell that he once bought a flageolet but he never made out a tune. Kavanagh got little further with the pipe, though he could always sing a ballad.

On a more serious level both men had a dislike of growing old and a sensitivity about their age and birthdays. Johnson disliked having his birthday mentioned and had a horror of old age. Kavanagh was evasive about his age and resented enquiries. 'I'm like a woman, when it comes to my age,' he told the Bellman. 'Any answer I'd give you would be bound to be a lie.' [25]

This extended comparison with Johnson may help to illuminate the character and personality of Kavanagh, but the comparison must not be pressed too far. The differences between eighteenth century London and twentieth century Dublin are great, even though McDaid's Bar may have some shadowy resemblance to the Mitre Tavern. Johnson was more fortunate than Kavanagh in his literary milieu. He was the leading member of a dominant literary group, an 'in-group'. This gave him stability, confidence, ease. Kavanagh remained something of an outsider. Although he spoke with an authority accepted by many and his work was praised and admired, he lacked the security of an accepted literary milieu. He was a more lonely figure than Johnson.

Yeats believed that the poet needed masks. He felt that he could not speak directly as to someone at the breakfast table. In his poetry his own face must be covered. 'I commit my emotion to shepherds, herdsmen, camel-drivers, learned men, Milton's or Shelley's Platonist, that tower Palmer drew.' [26] When the poet wears a mask, he is inevitably somewhat withdrawn as a man, and this seems to have been true of Yeats. This does not mean that Yeats was insincere, but he had something of a public voice and manner that kept him aloof.

Most of us wear something of a social mask to protect us from the gaze of strangers. But Kavanagh always abjured masks and protective disguises. He spoke as he felt, even when it would embarrass and offend. He resisted all attempts to fix on him a persona, to make him conform to a role. His hatred of cant led him to reject polite evasions and compromises and even good manners. As a film critic he refused to leave his 'poetic soul' at home and raged against 'this Jekyll and Hyde segregation of spiritual and mental attributes, this expediency to suit the occasion'. [27]

In many ways Kavanagh was a man of passionate sincerity and honesty, to the point of offensiveness. There is a passage in George Moore's *Vale,* where he is discussing the exemption of the artist from good manners, that throws light on Kavanagh's personality.

Well-mannered people do not think sincerely, their minds are full of evasions and subterfuges. Well-mannered people

102

constantly feel that they would not like to think like this or that, and whosoever feels that he would not like to think out to the end every thought that may come into his mind should turn from Parnassus. In his search for new formulas, new moulds, all the old values must be swept aside. The artist must arrive at a new estimate of things; all must go into the melting-pot in the hope that out of the pot may emerge a new consummation of himself. For this end he must keep himself free from all creed, from all dogma, from all opinion, remembering that as he accepts the opinions of others he loses his talent, all his feelings and his ideas must be his own, for Art is a personal rethinking of life from end to end, and for this reason the artist is always eccentric.[28]

W. H. Auden was thinking along the same lines as George Moore when he remarked that: 'Only a minor talent can be a perfect gentleman.' [29]

Kavanagh neither was nor aspired to be 'a perfect gentleman'. It does not follow that he can be comfortably classified as 'an eccentric'. Moore in fact does not use the indefinite article. He only observes that the artist is 'eccentric', outside the accepted centre, following his own ideas and feelings wherever they lead him.

In a moment of remarkable self-awareness and self-acceptance Kavangh wrote a poem entitled 'The Gift'. He reveals in it how his own longing for a smooth perfection is mistaken. God can only give him himself: for him perfection, wisdom, comfort, would be death.

> One day I asked God to give
> Me perfection so I'd live
> Smooth and courteous, calmly wise
> All the world's virtuous prize.
>
> So I should not always be
> Getting into jeopardy,
> Being savage, wild and proud
> Fighting, arguing with the crowd;
>
> Being poor, sick, depressed,
> Everywhere an awful pest;
> Being too right, being too wrong,
> Being too weak, being too strong.

Being every hour fated
To say the things that make me hated;
Being a failure in the end —
God, perfection on me spend.

And God spoke out of Heaven
The only gift in My giving
Is yours — Life. Seek in hell
Death, perfect, wise, comfortable.

Kavanagh was certainly a sincere and honest writer, and yet he
himself qualified this view.

People have always accused me of passionate honesty, of an
unworldliness that couldn't be trained to keep a shut mouth.
I have often tried hard to explain that I am not that honest,
but it's no use.[30]

There was an unworldliness about Kavanagh, but it was not a
simple saintly unworldliness. It often spoilt his chances of 'getting
on', and yet he had a keen awareness of the value of money. He
often discussed the economic circumstances of writers and he
revealed a certain envy of financial success. Nor was he indifferent
to public opinion in spite of his apparent contempt of it. This is
shown by his libel action against the *Leader*. A completely simple
and unworldly man would not have undertaken this. He referred
to himself as an 'abnormally normal' man, and when, in declining
to accept the role of hero, of poet-genius, he told his admirers

I am as obvious as an auctioneer
Dreaming of twenty thousand pounds a year . . .

this is not simply evasive irony. He was speaking of himself when
he told his students at University College, Dublin: 'the creative
genius has one constant dream, to have a large public and to be
corrupted.'[31]

His sincerity and outspokeness, his 'kink of rectitude', was both
strength and weakness. He himself acknowledged this in a revealing
dialogue with himself in one of his *Envoy* diaries.

If you wanted to make money you could make it, as Ethel
Manin has told you. You have a touch which can make you

104

the most popular writer this country has produced. I partly agree but something always prevents me realising it.

A defect of character, my friend; you've had it since you were not (as country phrase has it) "two hands high over a hen". It is hard to define this defect of yours, which is actually the source of your attraction. It is an innocence of heart but it is a feckless quality too. It produces pride, covetousness, lust, gluttony, envy, anger and sloth.[32]

There was in Kavanagh, as there was in Johnson, a basic innocence of heart. But a fecklessness went with it that the stabler and more fortunate Johnson was free from. Kavanagh had the originality and the force of genius. He had the eccentricity, the lack of self-confidence and self-control that marked him as a man who once stood outside, lost in the fog.

8

RELUCTANT HARVEST

After the publication of *Come Dance with Kitty Stobling* Kavanagh contributed only a few poems to literary journals, but in 1964 his *Collected Poems* appeared in a handsome volume from MacGibbon and Kee. This contained most, but by no means all, of his previously published poetry. Kavanagh's own somewhat strange attitude to the collection is revealed in the short preface.

> Besides *The Great Hunger* there are many poems in this collection which I dislike; but I was too indifferent, too lazy to eliminate, change or collect.

As with his attitude to his own countryside, so with his attitude to his own poetry, there is a persistent ambivalence; he is indifferent and yet concerned, he loves and hates. At the beginning of his broadcast script, 'An Inspired Idiot', he said: 'Any verse of mine over a week old bores me stiff. I am only interested in what I have written to-day or may write to-morrow.' [1]

This impatience with finished work is a perfectly natural and comprehensible feeling for a creative writer to have. It did not, of course, mean that he would never look again at what he had written, never revise past work. He does in fact frequently quote from his own past work in his newspaper columns and elsewhere. He sometimes worked at revision of earlier verse, and the poems in the collected edition are by no means exactly as first published in journals.

Had the collection been left to Kavanagh himself it would have been very incomplete. He was not an easy man for publishers to deal with. It was due mainly to the enthusiasm of Martin Green and Timothy O'Keeffe that a collection was made at all. Kavanagh handed in a meagre typescript that included nothing from his early volumes, *A Ploughman and Other Poems* and *A Soul for Sale,* not even 'The Great Hunger'. The poet, John Montague, who knew Kavanagh's work well, was enlisted to help enlarge the collection and he is largely responsible for the first half of the book as it is.

It was not in Kavanagh's temperament to look after his own work. He sometimes lost and mislaid his poems. The poem entitled 'Thank You, Thank You', designed as an epilogue to a series of lectures given at University College, Dublin, in 1956, provides an example. The printed poem is only a fragment. Kavanagh said of it: 'I found on my floor the bottom half of this poem. The beginning and the middle are "irretrievably" lost.' [2]

Another example of a fragmentary piece is 'Cyrano de Bergerac'. As it is printed in *Collected Poems* this contains two and a half verses of the original four first published in *The Bell*[3] and it hardly makes sense. It is quite likely that Kavanagh had lost or mislaid the second page of the typescript.

It is hardly surprising then that the book is not a complete collection. At the same time it is not a selection, because it contains some of his worst poems. But it does include the bulk of Kavanagh's published poetry and it allows us to see his work in perspective. There is a great difference between the beginning and the end of the book; there is considerable variety of style and mood, and there is striking unevenness of achievement.

Broadly speaking, Kavanagh's weakest poems come at the beginning and end of his career as a poet. Since he had as early models the verse corner of an Irish Sunday newspaper and the thin romantic-pastoral diet of minor Georgian poets, it is not surprising that many of his early poems are weak. The carelessness and indifference in some of his later verse is not due to incompetence or bad models; it is deliberate.

'Anyhow, I did arrive at complete casualness, at being able to play a true note on a dead slack string',[4] Kavanagh remarked in *Self-Portrait*. This casual manner was something he valued and cultivated. We find it, for example, in 'Literary Adventures', which he quoted in *Self-Portrait*.

> I am here in a garage in Monaghan
> It is June and the weather is warm,
> Just a little bit cloudy. There's the sun again
> Lifting to importance my sixteen acre farm.

Here the manner is successful; the tone is easy, relaxed and yet the words are communicating what he wants them to communicate.

But some of the casual poems give an impression of carelessness and clumsiness rather than colloquial ease. Kavanagh leaned over backwards in an effort to avoid solemnity and respectability. 'One of the good ways of getting out of this respectability,' he wrote, 'is the judicious use of slang and outrageous rhyming.' [5] But such usage must be judicious if it is to succeed. Some of the poems seem to me to avoid one kind of 'ponderosity' only to fall into another. An example of this is 'The Gambler: A Ballet with Words'. It is not sufficiently light and amusing to carry off its outrageous rhymes, in an Ogden Nash manner, nor has it sufficient poetic pressure to be effective on a more serious level. Here is a passage from the opening 'Explanation'.

> For the artifice cold and implacable
> Has an inhuman beauty for our pleasure
> The dancers are a veritable treasure
> In a world so noisily cacable.
> From a normal viewpoint they are untackable
> Stylised sex sinful but unbackable
> Essentially as toys meant
> Unlike Annie Besant
> Whose backside was quite whackable
> When we want to be withdrawn they are the answer
> To many problems in a television society.
> You are in a low pub reading the paper
> And you see in the monstrous mirrors the sleething dancer
> Who demands of you no emotional moiety
> Of your attention as he capes his caper.

The rhymes are certainly outrageous; but they call attention to themselves for no particular reason. The reader becomes more conscious of the language than of the statement made.

Kavanagh once remarked during an interview that: 'Poetry is not really an art. It's only saying things.' [6] The remark illuminates the difference between his approach to writing and that of Yeats who wanted his words to sing and dance, or to have the cold beauty of sculptured stone. 'Words alone are certain good.' Yeats falls over into rhetoric; Kavanagh falls over into doggerel. Yeats would never have used words like 'anti-dignity', 'unhard' and 'unselectual'. Kavanagh doesn't care if he forces a rhyme in the most amateur way.

The old canal is as full of blue sky
As a year ago and so kind to I.

Dismissed a dead loss in the final up toss.

In the *Collected Poems* the satirical poems are grouped together at the beginning of Section IV. This affords the reader an opportunity to consider Kavanagh's work as a verse satrist. It might be expected that he would excel in satire He had a reputation for destructive wit and he had a passionate hatred of many things. But in fact, with a few exceptions, his satiric poems seem to me the least rewarding to the reader.

There are two sustained satires on the Dublin literary and cultural world, 'The Paddiad' and 'Adventures in the Bohemian Jungle'. 'The Paddiad', or the Devil as a Patron of Irish Letters, is an attack on a literary group in Dublin which is promoting a bogus renaissance in Irish letters. When the poem was published in *Come Dance with Kitty Stobling* Kavanagh included an apologetic explanatory note to warn the reader that it was based on 'false and ridiculous premises', on 'the sad notion with which my youth was infected that Ireland was a spiritual entity'.

The devil of the poem is a mild literary dictator 'the master of the mediocre', who dispenses praise to the literary Paddies gathered round him:

In their middle sits a fellow
Aged about sixty, bland and mellow;
Saintly, silvery locks of hair,
Quiet-voiced as monk at prayer. . . .
Far and near he screws his eyes
In search of what will never rise,
Souls that are fusty, safe and dim,
These are the geniuses of the land to him.

Into this circle intrudes Paddy Conscience, 'a man who looks the conventional devil.', a half-drunk, dirty, disreputable poet, with 'a dangerous arrogance'. This is clearly Paddy Kavanagh himself. In the course of the poem he is chucked out of the bar and soon news comes of his death in Paris. The devil speaks ingratiatingly of his genius, ready to gather him into the fold of Irish letters, now that he is safely dead.

109

The Emerald Isle
Must bury him in tourist style.

The verse is clever and amusing, but it is difficult to accept
Kavanagh's terms of reference. The satire is too personal, insufficiently distanced and detached. The same weakness is found, to a
much greater degree, in 'Adventures in the Bohemian Jungle'.
Again Kavanagh himself, as the simple Countryman, is too nearly
involved in the poem. The waters of satire are muddied by personal
rancour; there is insufficient distillation. The satire is too gross,
too simple, without any real laughter. At times the tone is almost
embarrassing.

From the depths of the rotten vegetation can be heard the
screams of drunken girls.

A greater detachment in the tone of 'House Party to Celebrate the
Destruction of the Roman Catholic Church in Ireland' makes this
a much more successful poem. Kavanagh does not appear himself
and his method of satire has more subtlety. I like best the last three
lines, where the shallow triumph of the liberal intellectual is con-
trasted with the dignity of the threatened church.

In far off parishes of Cork and Kerry,
Old priests walked homeless in the winter air
As Seamus poured another pale dry sherry.

The irony in these lines is as dry as the sherry; whereas in the
'Bohemian Jungle' everything is damp.
   Another satire that is successful, in spite of the fact that the
theme is now somewhat worn, is 'Who killed James Joyce?' Here
again the tone is dry and detached.

Who killed James Joyce?
I, said the commentator,
I killed James Joyce
For my graduation.

What weapon was used
To slay mighty Ulysses?
The weapon that was used
Was a Harvard thesis. . . .

With one or two fine exceptions Kavanagh is not at his best in
straight satire. He himself remarked in 'Prelude', where he deplores
'that angry bitter look',

> But satire is unfruitful prayer
> Only wild shoots of pity there
> And you must go inland and be
> Lost in compassion's ecstasy.

And in 'Living in the Country:' he makes a solemn protestation
that his intention is

> — not satire but humaneness
> An eagerness to understand more about sad man . . .

'The Paddiad' and 'Adventures in the Bohemian Jungle' belong to
the period before the hegira on the canal bank and the serenity that
came with 'not caring'.

Even when his main intention is not satire, a satiric edge gives
cutting power to much of Kavanagh's poetry. In 'Father Mat' the
figure of the old priest is conveyed with sympathy, but there is a
sharp satiric sketch of his young curate.

> His curate passed on a bicycle —
> *He* had the haughty intellectual look
> Of the man who never reads in brook or book;
> A man designed to wear a mitre,
> To sit on committees —
> For will grows strongest in the emptiest mind.
> The old priest saw him pass
> And, seeing, saw
> Himself a medieval ghost.
> Ahead of him went Power,
> One who was not afraid when the sun opened a flower,
> Who was never astonished
> At a stick carried down a stream
> Or at the undying difference in the corner of a field.

Except in the very early romantic poems, irony is an ingredient
of all Kavanagh's poetry, seasoning and sharpening its flavour. It

is present in 'The Great Hunger' and we find it in 'In Blinking Blankness', the last poem to appear in *Collected Poems*. Here he turns the irony against himself as he often does.

> Nature is not enough, I've used up lanes
> Waters that run in rivers or are stagnant.

One of his finest ironic poems is a comparatively early one, 'A Wreath for Tom Moore's Statue', first published in the *Irish Times* in 1944.[7] This could be called a satire; the first two verses are certainly satire, but the last verse flows into hope and vision. When the poem first appeared it bore the title 'Statue, Symbol and Poet' and the note underneath it in brackets 'Not concerning Thomas Moore'. I interpret this to mean that Kavanagh was not considering the individual poet, Tom Moore, but simply the general tendency to corrupt the reality of the poet by worshipping a false image of him. Moore's statue, an uninspiring piece of sculpture, becomes a symbol of the way the false figure replaces the true. When a poet is dead he is safe. He can no longer disturb or protest. 'The corpse can be fitted out to deceive' and he cannot disown 'the cap of any racket'. And so —

> No poet's honoured when they wreathe this stone,
> An old shop-keeper who has dealt in the marrow-bone
> Of his neighbours looks at you.
> Dim-eyed, degenerate, he is admiring his god,
> The bank-manager who pays his monthly confession,
> The tedious narrative of a mediocrity's passion,
> The shallow, safe sins that never become a flood
> To sweep themselves away . . .

The wreath is offered, not to the poet, but to death,

>   the old reliable
> Whose white blood cannot blot the respectable page.

But paying tributes to death and respectability cannot prevent the new seed of poetry from springing up again and again. The destructive irony changes to hope.

But hope! the poet comes again to build
A new city high above lust and logic,
The trucks of language overflow and magic
At every turn of the living road is spilled.

Magic is not always spilled from Kavanagh's trucks of language, but when we have discounted the weak and ineffective verse — perhaps more than half the book — we are left with enough genuine and original poetry to earn him an honorable place amongst the poets of the twentieth century. I have already discussed in earlier chapters the poetry that seems to me the best; in brief, the Monaghan poems and the poems of the Canal Bank period. Most of these are in the *Collected Poems,* and they demonstrate a remarkable thing, that after all the years that have passed since Wordsworth made nature worship fashionable, after all the clichés about the 'beauties of nature' and the 'good earth', a twentieth century poet can still write about the country with freshness and vitality. At his best Kavanagh does just this, and part of his strength lies in the fact that his vision of rural life is never divorced from common reality. His feet are firmly planted in the clay and dung, and yet, in the midst of the commonplace, he perceives those 'bright shoots of everlastingness' that Vaughan knew.

At the same time his bright shoots are by no means found only in the country. The Canal Bank poems belong to Dublin, even if there are glances back at Monaghan; and some of the successful personal poems have no particular location. The *Collected Poems* reveal a poet, not simply a country or peasant poet.

9

AFTER THE HARVEST

In the years after the publication of *Collected Poems* Kavanagh did receive recognition and awards, but he had little time to enjoy the fruits of success. He first appeared in *Who's Who* in 1967, and that year he was awarded a poetry bursary by the Arts Council in London. In the same year he got married and he died. He married Katharine Barry Maloney on 19 April in Dublin. On 30 November he died of pneumonia in a Dublin nursing home. A funeral Mass was celebrated at St. Mary's Church, Haddington Road, attended by Ministers of State and other public figures. Afterwards his body was taken to Inniskeen and buried there at the parish church.

After Patrick's death his brother Peter published three volumes containing his work, under the imprint of the Peter Kavanagh Hand Press in New York. The first of these is entitled *Lapped Furrows* (1969) and it consists mainly of correspondence between Patrick and Peter during the years 1933 to 1967. There is also an introduction by Peter, containing some useful information about the family home in Inniskeen and a brief but attractive memoir of Patrick by his sister Celia, who entered a convent in England. The book contains a great deal of biographical interest but it hardly adds to Kavanagh's stature as a writer. As a correspondent he is too often laconic and slap dash.

November Haggard (1971) contains a selection, arranged and edited by Peter, of Patrick's hitherto uncollected prose and verse. The prose is drawn from articles in magazines and newspapers such as *Envoy* and the *Irish Farmer's Journal* and it supplements the earlier *Collected Pruse*. The poems are all supplementary to *Collected Poems*, the most interesting being the longest, 'Lough Derg', which I have discussed in Chapter 3. This book also contains an interesting collection of photographs including some early family ones.

Finally Peter gathered together all the poems, including the juvenilia, in *The Complete Poems of Patrick Kavanagh*. Future readers must be grateful for this collection even though there is much that is weak when his verse is presented in bulk. His reputation is likely to be best served by judicious selection; but of course we must have the material to select from.

In spite of winning considerable fame and influence Kavanagh remained on the defensive and somewhat aloof. He never became, like Yeats,

A sixty year old smiling public man.

Although he preached the doctrine of not caring, he did not find it easy to relax; he was never completely at ease on Parnassus. This may help to explain his strange attitude to his own work. Many writers deplore some of their own early work, often because their attitudes have changed, but Kavanagh persisted in denigrating a great deal of his own work. In the preface to *Collected Poems,* he remarks: 'I would not object if some critic said I was not a poet at all.' He dismissed *The Green Fool,* he disliked *The Great Hunger* and he rejected most of the poems written before 1955.

Dr. Johnson once observed: 'All censure of a man's self is oblique praise. It is in order to show how much he can spare.'[1] There is undoubtedly a touch of arrogance in Kavanagh's condemnation of his own work but it would be too simple to see it merely as oblique self-praise. He was driven by a passionate hatred of pretence, pose, attitude. This explains his dislike of *The Great Hunger.*

In *The Great Hunger,* d'you see, you get this great concern for the woes of the poor — the social land; it is far too strong for honesty. And can a thing be truly compassionate if it is touched with hypocrisy?[2]

The great poetic virtue for Kavanagh was to be true to one's own feeling and experience, even if it seemed like selfishness. He steadfastly refused to pay tribute to any cause or movement, doctrine or ideology. In his poem, 'No Social Conscience', he is describing himself.

He was an egoist with an unsocial conscience,
And I liked him for it though he was out of favour,
For he seemed to me to be sincere,
Wanting to be no one's but his own saviour.

115

Kavanagh was never a poet with a mask. He was always patently and blatantly himself. This was his strength, but also his weakness. It might be said that Yeats found a new energy in his old age by discarding masks and disguises, by dismissing his circus animals.

> Now that my ladder's gone
> I must lie down where all the ladders start,
> In the foul rag-and-bone shop of the heart.

Kavanagh had no masks to discard, no 'players and painted stage' to dismiss. When personal vision failed him, there was nothing for him to fall back on, no mythology, no service to cause or craft to sustain him. In his last years his occasional poems express a sense of loss; the page before him is blank and inspiration flags:

> Nature is not enough, I've used up lanes
> Waters that run in rivers or are stagnant;
> But I have no message and the sins
> Of no red idea can make me pregnant.

'In Blinking Blankness', 'On Rampas Point', and 'Personal Problem' all suggest a drying up of poetic springs, an exhaustion of spiritual energy. In 'Personal Problem' he complains again that he lacks a subject.

> If I could rewrite a famous tale
> Or perhaps return to a midnight calving,
> This cow sacred on a Hindu scale —
> So there it is my friends. What am I to do
> With the void growing more awful every hour?
> I lacked a classical discipline. I grew
> Uncultivated and now the soil turns sour . . .

The same harsh honesty distinguishes these few last poems; and it must surely be counted to Kavanagh's credit that he did not flog a sour soil to produce more verse in his last years.

It is only fair to judge a poet by his best work. I have already indicated that, in my opinion, the best poems are the 'Monaghan' poems, including, of course, *The Great Hunger,* and the Canal Bank poems, including the gay and jaunty personal poems that appeared with them in *Come Dance with Kitty Stobling.* To these I would add a few of the very early poems and some of the very

116

late ones. On the basis of these poems, about a third of those included in *Collected Poems,* what conclusions can we come to about Kavanagh's poetry, and his standing as an Irish poet of the twentieth century?

Frank O'Connor sees him as one of 'the strayed revellers of the Irish literary revival'.[3] But it seems to me that Kavanagh stands clearly outside any literary or cultural revival and outside the nationalist enthusiasms of the early twentieth century. He speaks for an Ireland that has little relation to the 'peasant quality' cultivated by Yeats and Synge and the Abbey Theatre. There are no legendary heroes in his writings, such as Cuchulainn or Deirdre, no Celtic gods, no leprecauns, no Celtic Twilight at all. At the same time there is very little consciousness of political or cultural nationalism. His Ireland is not the Ireland of Patrick Pearse and the men of 1916. Although he himself belonged to the Sinn Fein party and tried unsuccessfully to join the I.R.A., the political fervour of the times left no mark on him. 'In spite of all the loud glory and movement of those years, I count them among the lost years of my life.' [4]

Kavanagh speaks out of an Irish world that is older and more enduring than the world of the literary revival and the 'Troubles'. It is less exciting, perhaps, more monotonously bound to clay and bog, but it reaches back to Carleton and the times before the Famine, and it still lives on in the back parts of the prosperous, go-getting, bourgeois economy of modern Ireland. It is the world of hens and donkeys in the backyard, of the broken straw-stuffed straddle and the old plough upside down on a weedy ridge. In this world people still carry water from the well and gossip over their gates, using well-worn traditional phrases.

As a poet of the countryside Kavanagh sticks close to country tasks, but he is not simply the faithful delineator of a humble rural world. He is a poet of vision, who, like Tarry Flynn, has seen the 'ecstatic light of Life in stones, on the hills, in leaves of cabbages and weeds'.[5] At bottom he is a religious poet, who finds the Holy Spirit flowering in the ditches and in the neglected corners of the fields. In his best moments he experienced an outflowing of love for the familiar scenes and humble objects around him. As he says of Tarry, 'something happened when [he] looked at a flower or a stone in a ditch'.[6] A similar kind of experience

117

happened to Gerard Manly Hopkins when he looked at a bluebell. 'I know the beauty of Our Lord by it',[7] he wrote in his journal. Hopkins looks with the more detached eye of the pictorial as well as the verbal artist. He was sketching the bluebell and observing its exact 'inscape'. Kavanagh is more aware of his own feelings, of the strength of the love and wonder that fill his being.

Standing on the side of a hill in Monaghan, an indifferent landscape of crooked lanes and little humpy hills covered with whins, I found love, the kind of love that purifies, a sort of Divine love.[8]

There is clearly a strong vein of mysticism in Kavanagh's experience and the poetry that records it. Since the realm of mystical experience is a cloudy and ill-defined one, it may help to quote a working definition suggested by W. H. Auden.

All experiences which may be called mystical have certain characteristics in common. First the experience is given. It cannot be induced or prolonged under effort and will, though the openness of any individual to receiving it may be affected by age, by psychophysical make up, and by cultural milieu. Secondly, whatever the contents of the experience the subject is absolutely convinced that it is a revelation of reality. That is to say, when it is over, he does not say, as one says when one wakes from a dream: 'Now I am awake and aware of the real world.' He says: 'For a while reality was revealed to me, which in my normal state is hidden from me.' Thirdly, with whatever the experience is concerned — things, or human beings, or God — they are experiences as numinous, clothed in glory, charged with an intensity of being, an intense being — thereness. Lastly, the experience is so important that it completely absorbs the attention of the subject, so that his self, with its desires and needs, is of no importance whatsoever. While the visions last his self is completely forgotten or annihilated.[9]

If we press the analogy between religion and poetry too hard we shall be guilty of what Kavanagh would call 'ponderosity', but the four characteristics mentioned here by Auden do seem to fit very aptly the experience that lies behind the best of Kavanagh's poetry.

He would certainly have agreed that the experience was 'given'. As he says himself:

> God cannot catch us
> Unless we stay in the unconscious room
> Of our hearts.

There is no doubt about his strong conviction of the reality and importance of his experiences, and the 'intense being-thereness' is one of the things his poetry conveys to us. It is found in his childhood memories of Christmas and in the reactions of the middle-aged convalescent poet to the 'inexhaustible adventure of a gravelled yard.'

Kavanagh, like many other poets, is more concerned with his relationship to the universe, to God and to the Spirit of Place, than he is with human relationships. After one of his returns to Monaghan he remarks:

> I think now that the Spirit of Place has a more powerful attraction for us than friends or relations. . . . A tree, a stone or a field recreates for us the happiest — and the saddest, which is the same thing — moments of our lives — in other words, our moments of most intense experience.[10]

In one of the later poems, 'Question to Life', he asks if his passion is to be limited to inanimate nature and gives his own answer.

> Surely you would not ask me to have known
> Only the passion of primrose banks in May
> Which are merely a point of departure for the play
> And yearning poignancy when on their own.
> Yet when all is said and done a considerable
> Portion of living is found in inanimate
> Nature, and a man need not feel miserable
> If fate should have decided on this plan of it.

The questioning of life in this poem is not querulous or sour. The emphasis is on acceptance and praise.

Kavanagh only rarely writes poems about other people; he has no bent towards the character sketch or the dramatic monologue. Although he frequently indicates his regard for women, and makes references to loves gained and missed, he rarely celebrates sexual love. The attitude expressed in 'One Wet Summer', expressed with remarkable candour and honesty, is revealing.

> As it is I praise the rain
> For washing out the bank holiday with its moral risks
> It is not a nice attitude but it is conditioned by circumstances
> And by a childhood perverted by Christian moralists.

The outgoing of love in Kavanagh's poetry is more often towards things than people. This may be a limitation, but it is one also found in Wordsworth, to go no further. It should not make us under-estimate the energy and intensity of the love that is expressed. What is striking about Kavanagh's reply to his own question is the emphasis on praise:

> . . . praise, praise praise
> The way it happened and the way it is.

'There can be no good literature without praise',[11] said Yeats, and Kavanagh would have agreed with him. He stated in the last number of *Kavanagh's Weekly* that the purpose of the poet is to give people an enthusiasm for life. This enthusiasm is notably absent from the poetry of many of Kavanagh's contemporaries. There is little of it, for instance, in the work of Philip Larkin, a poet much better known to readers of poetry than Kavanagh. Much of Larkin's poetry suggests a distaste for life.

> Life is first boredom, then fear.
> Whether or not we use it, it goes,
> And leaves what something hidden from us chose,
> And age, and then the only end of age.

In spite of unevenness and occasional sourness, in spite of some-times shouting 'praise' and 'beauty', instead of revealing and pre-senting them, Kavanagh does kindle once more the reader's en-thusiasm for life. He does, in Wordsworth's phrase, 'reinvest with spirituality the material universe', and lead us back to

> The placeless heaven that's under all our noses.

At the end of one of his lectures to the students at University College, Dublin, Kavanagh remarked:

A few lines is all that the best of us has to bequeathe to the coming generation. That is why the best poets are seldom what is called Men of Letters: they live their lives because this attitude within them keeps them apart from the world of letters and its futile fertility.[12]

Whether or not the best poets can be found within the ranks of the Men of Letters is infinitely arguable. Johnson, Milton, Pope, Wordsworth, Coleridge, Arnold, T. S. Eliot and W. B. Yeats are all indisputably Men of Letters. Shakespeare, Burns, Clare, Dylan Thomas and D. H. Lawrence are not; but it is difficult to prove anything from tables of this sort. It is almost impossible to define a Man of Letters. In spite of this, all who read him will agree that Kavanagh is right to exclude himself from the world of letters. He is defining the truth of poetry for himself. He was never in danger from the 'futile fertility' he speaks of. But he has bequeathed to the future the few lines that matter; in a hundred years or so someone will still be reading some of them.

PATRICK KAVANAGH
A CHECKLIST

A. *Published Works*

1 PLOUGHMAN AND OTHER POEMS. Patrick Kavanagh. Macmillan's Contemporary Poets. Macmillan & Co. Ltd., London 1936. Thirty one poems. 8vo. 36 pp. Blue wrappers.

2 THE GREEN FOOL. Patrick Kavanagh. Michael Joseph Ltd., London 1938. Fictional autobiography. First edition 8vo. 350 pp. Green cloth.

3 — ditto. Second edition. Harper and Brothers, New York and London 1939. Printed in Great Britain.

4 THE GREAT HUNGER.* Patrick Kavanagh. The Cuala Press, Dublin 1942. Narrative poem. 8vo. 36 pp. Linen spine with blue-grey boards. Edition limited to 250 copies.

5 — ditto. MacGibbon & Kee, London 1966. Green paper covers. This is an offprint from the text in *Collected Poems* (No. 15).

6 A SOUL FOR SALE. Macmillan & Co. Ltd., London 1947. Nineteen poems, including *The Great Hunger* (with a part of Section II omitted). 8vo. 55 pp. Green cloth.

7 TARRY FLYNN. The Pilot Press, London 1948. Autobiographical novel. 8vo. 195 pp. Orange cloth.

8 — ditto. Devin Adair Co., New York 1949. 8vo. 256 pp. Olive cloth.

9 — ditto. New English Library Ltd., London 1962. Four Square books, paperback edition. 192 pp.

The Great Hunger is also published in *Longer Contemporary Poems*, ed. David Wright, Penguin 1966.

10 — ditto. MacGibbon & Kee, London 1965. 8vo. 256 pp. Brown boards. This is identical with the 1949 New York edition.

11 — ditto. Mayflower Books, London 1969.

12 KAVANAGH'S WEEKLY. Dublin 1952. Weekly magazine, 12 April – 15 July (13 issues). Published at 62, Pembroke Road.

13 RECENT POEMS. Patrick Kavanagh. Peter Kavanagh Hand Press, New York 1958. 4to. 28 pp. Hand set in 12 pt. Egmont Light. 25 copies.

14 COME DANCE WITH KITTY STOBLING and other poems. Patrick Kavanagh. Longmans, Green & Co. Ltd., London 1960. Thirty-five poems. 8vo. 44 pp. Brown cloth. Lettered in gold on upper board and on spine. Choice of the Poetry Book Society, Summer 1960.

15 SELF PORTRAIT. Patrick Kavanagh. The Dolmen Press, Dublin 1964. Photographs by Liam Miller. Text of a televised autobiographical discourse given by Patrick Kavanagh on Telefís Eireann in 1962. 31 pp. Green paper boards. Lettered on spine.

16 — ditto. The Dolmen Press, Dublin 1973. Paperback reissue of sheets of first edition.

17 COLLECTED POEMS. Patrick Kavanagh. MacGibbon & Kee, London 1964. Containing most, but not all of the published poems. 202 pp. Sand-coloured cloth lettered with gold on spine. A limited signed edition of 100 copies was quarter bound in green leather.

18 — ditto. Devin Adair Co., New York 1964. Rust coloured cloth. Black spine lettered in gold.

19 — ditto. Martin, Brian and O'Keeffe. Paperback, 1972.

20 COLLECTED PRUSE. Patrick Kavanagh. MacGibbon & Kee, London 1967.
Containing *Self Portrait*; a condensed version from the *Irish Times* of the trial in Dublin in February 1954 that followed Kavanagh's libel action against *The Leader*; extracts from

Tarry Flynn; articles from magazines and newspapers. Olive cloth lettered with gold on spine.

21   — ditto. Martin, Brian and O'Keeffe. Maroon boards lettered with gold on spine.

22   LAPPED FURROWS. Correspondence 1933–1967 between Patrick and Peter Kavanagh: with other documents. Edited by Peter Kavanagh. The Peter Kavanagh Hand Press, 250 East 30th Street, New York 10016, 1969. Pale brown cloth lettered with gold on spine.

23   NOVEMBER HAGGARD. Uncollected Prose and Verse of Patrick Kavanagh, selected, arranged and edited by Peter Kavanagh. The Peter Kavanagh Hand Press, New York, 1971. Pale blue cloth lettered with gold on spine.

24   THE COMPLETE POEMS OF PATRICK KAVANAGH. Collected, arranged and edited by Peter Kavanagh. The Peter Kavanagh Hand Press, New York, 1972. Dark green cloth lettered with gold on spine.

B. *Contributions to Books and Literary Journals*

HORIZON — January 1942.
   THE OLD PEASANT. First part of *The Great Hunger*.

IRISH WRITING (DUBLIN).
   No. 3, Nov. 1947,
      'F. R. Higgins; The Gallivanting Poet.'

THE BELL (DUBLIN).
   Vol. XV. 2 Nov. 1947,
      'The Wake of the Books. A Mummery.'
   XV. 3 December 1947,
      'Coloured Balloons: A Study of Frank O'Connor.'
   XVI. 1 April 1948,
      'Poetry in Ireland Today.'
   XVII. 5 August 1951,
      'Three pieces from a Novel.'
   XVIII. 11. Summer 1953,
      'A Goat Tethered Outside the Bailey.' Radio Talk.

XIX 4. March 1954,
  'Pages from a Literary Novel.'
XIX 5. April 1954,
  'Return in Harvest.' Radio Script.

NIMBUS (LONDON).
  Vol. III, No. 3, Summer 1956,
  'A Letter and an Environment from Dublin.'

STUDIES (DUBLIN).
  Spring 1959,
  'From Monaghan to the Grand Canal.'

ENVOY (DUBLIN).
  Nos. 1–20. December 1949 – July 1951,
  Monthly Diary.
  No. 19, June 1951,
  'Auden and the Creative Mind.'

X (LONDON).
  Vol. I No.   1961, 'Poets on Poetry' I.
      I No.   'The Flying Moment.'
      II No. 2. 'On a liberal Education.'
      II No. 3. 'The Cattle Fair.'

NONPLUS (DUBLIN).
  No. I, October 1959,
    'Nationalism and Literature.'
    'Violence and Literature.'
    'Suffering and Literature.'
  No. 2,
    'The G.A.A.'

NATIONAL OBSERVER (Dublin Monthly).
  Vol. 1, No. 3, Sept. 1958,
    'The Death of Nationalism.'
    Monthly column from July 1959 to January 1960.

ST. STEPHEN'S MAGAZINE.
(College Magazine published at University College, Dublin.)
  Trinity Term, 1962,
    'Writer at Work.'

'A Word of Sensibility', epilogue contributed to *Irish Mythology : a Dictionary* compiled by Peter Kavanagh, The Peter Kavanagh Hand Press, 1959.
Preface to W. STEURT TRENCH. *Realities of Irish Life.* MacGibbon & Kee. 1966.
Preface to *The Autobiography of William Carleton,* MacGibbon & Kee. 1968.

C. *Broadcasts*

BBC THIRD PROGRAMME, LONDON.
'Thinking of Other Things' (about Imagination, Childhood and London), 20 February 1951.
'Carleton and Irishness', 30 July 1951.
Introduction to a reading of 'The Great Hunger', 13 May 1960.
Discussion with Peter Duval-Smith. 'New Comment' Series, September 1964.

BBC WELSH REGION.
Discussion of Nationalism in Literature, 22 March 1963.

RADIO EIREANN.
'Looking Back', 14 September 1941.
'A Goat Tethered outside the Bailey', 2 February 1953.
'This is no Book', 17 September 1953.
'The Gambler', 23 September 1953.
'Return in Harvest', 1953.
'My Country Christmas', 24 December, 1953.
'A Hospital Notebook', 4 September 1955.

TELEFIS EIREANN.
Self-Portrait, 1962.
Image, 12 October 1964.

GRAMOPHONE RECORD
Almost Everything, Claddagh Records, Recorded 16 October 1963. Published April 1965.

D. *Bibliography*

Peter Kavanagh. *Garden of the Golden Apples.* A Bibliography of Patrick Kavanagh. Compiled and researched by Peter Kavanagh. The Peter Kavanagh Hand Press, 250 East 30th Street, New York 10016, 1972.

E. *Criticism and Comment. A Selection.*

THE BELLMAN.
'Meet Mr. Patrick Kavanagh', *The Bell,* Vol. XVI, No. 1, April 1948.

HUBERT BUTLER.
'Envoy and Mr. Kavanagh', *The Bell,* Vol. XVII, No. 6, September 1951.

JAMES PLUNKETT.
'Pulled Weeds on the Ridge', *The Bell,* Vol. XVII, No. 12, March 1952.

ANTHONY CRONIN.
'Innocence and Experience, The Poetry of Patrick Kavanagh', *Nimbus,* Vol. 3, No. 4, Winter 1956.

BASIL PAYNE.
'The Poetry of Patrick Kavanagh', *Studies,* Vol. XLIX, Autumn 1960.

JOHN JORDAN.
'Mr. Kavanagh's Progress', *Studies.* Vol. XLIX, Autumn 1960.

JOHN HEWITT.
'The Cobbler's Song'. *Threshold,* Vol. 5, No. 1, Spring/ Summer 1961.

PAUL POTTS.
'Patrick Kavanagh, The Poems and the Poet', *The London Magazine,* February 1963.

JOHN JORDAN.
'A Few Thoughts about P.K.', *Poetry Ireland,* No. 4, Summer 1964.

ALAN WARNER.
  'A Poet of the Countryside', *A Review of English Literature,*
  Vol. 5, No. 3, July 1964.

DOUGLAS SEALEY.
  'The Writings of Patrick Kavanagh', *The Dublin Magazine,*
  Vol. 4, Nos. 3 and 4, Autumn/Winter 1965.

J. M. NEWTON.
  'Patrick Kavanagh's Imagination', *Delta* (Cambridge), No. 37,
  Autumn 1965.

DAVID WRIGHT.
  'Patrick Kavanagh. 1905–1967', *The London Magazine.* New
  series, Vol. 8, No. 1, April 1968.

'A Tribute to Patrick Kavanagh', *The Dublin Magazine,* Vol. 7,
  No. 1, Spring 1968. Poems by Brendan Kennelly, Tom
  McGurk, Derek Mahon. Articles by Derek Mahon, Michael
  Longley, Alan Warner.

GRATTAN FREYER.
  'Patrick Kavanagh', *Eire — Ireland,* Vol. III, No. 4, Winter
  1968.

TOM McLAUGHLIN.
  'Patrick Kavanagh and the "Ireland" Myth', *The Honest
  Ulsterman,* No. 13, May 1969.

ALAN WARNER.
  'The Poet as Watcher', *Threshold,* (Belfast) No. 22, Summer
  1969.

ALAN WARNER.
  'The Poetry of Patrick Kavanagh (1904 - 1967)', *English,* Vol.
  XVIII, No. 102, Autumn 1969.

BRENDAN KENNELLY.
  'Patrick Kavanagh', *Ariel,* Vol. I, No. 3, July 1970.

FRANCIS BOYLAN.
  'Patrick Kavanagh'. *Ishmael* (Biarritz), Vol. I, No. 3, Winter-
  Spring 1972-3.

JAMES SIMMONS.
  'In Lieu of an Answer: Patrick Kavanagh's Poetry.' *The
  Honest Ulsterman,* No. 38, March/April/May, 1973.

A NOTE ON KAVANAGH'S POPULAR JOURNALISM

Irish Press (Dublin Daily).

City Commentary by Piers Plowman
14 Sept. 1942 – 8 Feb. 1944

This was a short column of personal comment; it usually appeared twice a week under the title of 'City Commentary', and it was signed 'Piers Plowman'. He adopted this pseudonym because Naomi Royde-Smith once compared him to Langland. 'Mr. Kavanagh and the author of *Piers Plowman* belong to the same spiritual age.'
He declared his aim in the first of his contributions.

> My object in writing these notes is to give a countryman's impressions of city life for the benefit of my friends in the country. I want to reveal in a simple way the usual — and unusual — life of the city: the Corporation workmen, the bus men, policemen, the civil servants, the theatres, Moore Street and also — what occupies so large a place in Dublin's life — the literary and artistic circles.

This series is the least interesting of Kavanagh's contributions to journalism. He himself later remarked: 'Looking back on that column I am afraid I must say that it was sticky and dull and they weren't too wrong when they fired me.' The notes are mostly only of passing interest, dealing briefly with events and people of the time, but occasionally a characteristic flash of Kavanagh humour or insight appears.

Irish Times (Dublin Daily).
Between 1942 and 1945 Kavanagh did a good deal of book reviewing for this newspaper. He was given a wide range of books to deal with, from *The Capuchin Annual* to the latest popular novel. He has some lively and amusing reviews of very inferior books.
He contributed some reflections on *Waiting for Godot* (28 June 1956) and an article for the Yeats Centenary Supplement on 'George Moore's Yeats' (10 June 1965).

The Standard (Dublin Weekly).

His main contribution to this paper was film criticism under the heading: 'Round the Cinemas with Patrick Kavanagh'. (22 February 1946 – 8 July 1949). He mostly dealt with films currently showing in Dublin but the film criticism is interspersed with remarks on various topics that occur to him, from original sin to the Irish landscape. He expresses fairly strong distaste for popular Hollywood films and also for continental 'Art' films.

He contributed a number of feature articles to this paper, most of them in 1942.

Irish Farmers' Journal (Dublin Weekly).

A regular personal column appearing in the 'Farm Home' section. 14 June 1958 – 9 March 1963.

Many of these articles are reminiscences of Kavanagh's country days, and they have been quoted at length in the early part of this book. A wide variety of other topics are covered, from cock-fighting to women's fashions and the theatre. The tone is mostly light-hearted, and he clearly intends to amuse and entertain. It is apparent that he frequently enjoyed writing this column. He once told the editor: 'There is nowhere in the world I feel half as much at home as in the Home Pages of the *Farmers' Journal*'. There is an element of good-humoured clowning in some of the articles, which are accompanied by comic cartoons of Kavanagh on a donkey, on a bicycle, digging spuds, even disguised as a bull. The style of the column is relaxed, easy, casual, at times careless.

RTV Guide (later this becomes *RTE Guide*).

This is the weekly programme magazine of Radio Telefis Eireann (Dublin); 5 April 1963 –16 June, 1967. Irregular; only occasional in later years.

This column began as film criticism; it was advertised as featuring 'the criticism and witticisms of Patrick Kavanagh'. But before long it became more general and it gradually turned into a brief personal column. There are flashes of wit and insight, some amusing anecdotes and interesting reminiscences, but in general the writing has neither the vitality of the earlier *Standard* film criticism, nor the gaiety of the page in the *Irish Farmers' Journal*. From time to time a certain sourness appears in his comments, especially those on established literary reputations. A weariness becomes evident, too.

Do you know, dear reader, that it is tough work
Keeping up a short weekly column? Did I
mention that before? May have. . . .
I am tired as I write this. And I must stop.

Note — A complete list of Kavanagh's newspaper articles may be found in his brother's bibliography, Peter Kavanagh: *Garden of the Golden Apples*. 1972.

APPENDIX
A LETTER FROM PAUL VINCENT CARROLL

Paul Vincent Carroll (1900–1968), the Irish playwright, was a friend of Kavanagh's in his youth. A common friend introduced them at Blackrock when Carroll was home from Glasgow on a holiday. Kavanagh records the friendship in *The Green Fool* and comments:

> With Paul Carroll I formed the warmest attachment which lasted for three years. It was indeed too warm, which was the cause of its disruption.

In 1964 I wrote to Carroll and he replied giving me his impressions of Kavanagh. The relevant part of the letter is published below, by kind permission of Miss Nancy Carroll and Mr. Malachy Carroll.

> 22 Park Road,
> Bromley,
> Kent.
> 15/1/64

Dear Professor Warner,

I have your letter which I much appreciate. Yes, I knew Patrick Kavanagh very well in the old days. He used to take his early poems to me at my mother's old place, written on the backs of envelopes. They had something in them that glowed with a strange light . . . (I was in Glasgow at that time, but used to spend a month or two with Mother). Patrick always had about him a sort of "original innocence" which was always reflected in his early poems. He was afraid — afraid of the sophisticated world he didn't know, and you will find this fear in his work, the fear of a child who puts its head under the blankets because it's afraid of the dark. He consoled himself in this fear by always addressing himself as "Child". Mark in his early poems:

> "Child, do not go into the dark places of soul,
> For there the grey wolves whine . . ."

Again,

"Child, there is light somewhere
Under a star . . ."

Again,

"Child, do not be afraid! . . .
These men know Christ. . . ."

At moments, with his fine head and glowing face and his great
lean height, he had in him a wisp of that unfathomable simplicity of Our Lord. He was as innocent as a child, and at the
same time as bucolic as a young bullock. His laugh in a pub,
terrific and uninhibited, had something of the ancient Fenians
in it. After all, Finn McCool was his neighbour on the Mourne
foothills.

When he asked my advice about going to Dublin, I felt
terribly sad and depressed. Having been "educated" early,
and knowing well the "grey wolves" of the Dublin writing
fraternity, I knew only too well what he would encounter in
jealousy and cunning! They were waiting for the kill! . . .
However, I gave him a little cash, and introductions to that
darling pagan saint, Æ, and the inimitable Bob Smyllie of the
Irish Times. I warned him of the pitfalls. I mightn't have
bothered my head — Patrick fell headlong into nearly all of
them. He even started putting on social "acts", just as the
contemporary Brendan Behan and his Bhoys are doing now.
The Great Hunger saved him, but only just! . . .

When I read a poem of his with the final couplet:

"And the maiden of Spring is with child
To the Holy Ghost . . . ,"

I knew for certain that here was a poet that might easily steal
the mantle that Æ passed on to Fred Higgins. I suffered Æ's
tea and plum duff one day in his studio, and asked him about
Patrick. Æ stroked the noble beard and said: "Any man who
can write that line, is a genius, even if the other lines are
dismissible. . . ." The line Æ referred to was:

"I find a star-lovely art in a dark sod. . . ."

Of course we mustn't forget that Æ was strongly pantheist

133

and that he tried to swing Patrick's mind towards Indian mysticism, which, with his own lovely Irish unfathomables, was unwise. . . . As you know, the death of Æ in 1937 was a major Irish tragedy conveniently overlooked by the gombeen men who ran the new Republic — in fact, in some respects a greater tragedy than the death of Yeats in 1939. . . . We began to descend. . . . One day at the Shelbourne I had two large whiskies with Fred Higgins. He told me he was finished and drank only lemonade. That evening he dropped dead outside of Jervis Street hospital. . . . The lament he composed for Padraic O'Conaire was recited over *his grave* instead of Padraic's! (The English would call that Irish!). But the mantle was Patrick's, had he been "clever" enough to have sized up the situation. To our mutual regret, he wasn't. . . . This stupid law suit, in which he was a sort of comic Aristophanes, delighted the charlatans of Dublin. They had him exactly where they wanted him. . . . He was "acting"! And Dublin loves actors. . . .

If you come to London in the summer and I am not in USA, come out to see me, and I'll tell you a lot about poor Patrick. I still think he is Ireland's finest poet! . . .

Sincerely,

P. V. Carroll

NOTES

Guide to abbreviations
C. Pr. Collected Pruse.
GF   The Green Fool
IFJ   The Irish Farmers' Journal.
KW   Kavanagh's Weekly.
SP   Self Portrait.
TF   Tarry Flynn.
Bos.   Boswell's Life of Johnson. Oxford University Press. 1933 (2 vols).

Notes to Preface
1 R.T.E. 12 August 1966.
2 W. H. Auden, 'In Memory of W. B. Yeats'.
3 'Return in Harvest'. *The Bell*, April 1954.

Chapter 1
1 IFJ 15 August 1960. A facsimile of the letter is printed in *November Haggard*.
2 *RTE Guide*, 4 March 1966.
3 GF, pp. 12–13.
4 IFJ, 17 February 1960.
5 IFJ, 3 June, 1961.
6 *Studies*, vol. 8, 1959, p. 29.
7 IFJ, 21 April 1962.
8 IFJ, 21 April, 1962.
9 IFJ, 15 November 1960. C. Pr. p. 50.
10 IFJ, 13 June 1961.
11 IFJ, 29 September 1962.
12 IFJ, 30 June 1962.
13 IFJ, 13 September 1958.
14 IFJ, 17 February 1962.
15 IFJ, 14 February 1959.
16 IFJ, 12 May 1962.
17 Peter Kavanagh: *Dictionary of Irish Mythology*, p. 147.
18 IFJ, 12 May 1962.
19 Poetry Book Society Bulletin, no. 25, June 1960.
20 IFJ, 12 September 1959.
21 SP, p. 9.
22 IFJ, 3 June 1961.
23 IFJ, 27 September 1958.
24 Sunday Times Illustrated Supplement, 31 May 1964.
25 *RTV Guide*, 16 December 1964.
26 IFJ, 24 October 1959.
27 KW, no. 5.
28 IFJ, 9 June 1962.
29 *RTV Guide*, 15 January 1965.

30 IFJ, 10 February 1962.
31 IFJ, 12 July 1958. See also C. Pr. p. 49.
32 *Irish Press,* 'City Commentary', 4 June 1943.
33 IFJ, 14 November 1959.
34 IFJ, 14 November 1959.
35 IFJ, 8 September 1962.
36 IFJ, 19 December 1959.
37 IFJ, 10 January 1959.
38 IFJ, 10 January 1959.
39 *Horizon,* vol. 5, 25 January 1942.
40 IFJ, 30 June 1959.

Chapter 2

1 *The Bell,* April 1948 p. 7.
2 *RTV Guide,* 7 August 1964.
3 IFJ, 6 September 1958.
4 GF, pp. 316–7.
5 GF, pp. 146–8.
6 GF, p. 209.
7 GF, pp. 194–6.
8 GF, p. 13.
9 GF, p. 135.
10 GF, pp. 326–8.
11 GF, p. 300.
12 *Irish Times,* 21 March 1939.
13 TF, pp. 11–12.
14 TF, p. 69.
15 TF, pp. 91–3.
16 TF, p. 63.
17 TF, pp. 40–1.
18 TF, pp. 126–7.
19 SP, p. 8.
20 *Delta* (Cambridge), no. 37. Autumn 1965.
21 TF, p. 188.
22 TF, p. 27.
23 TF, p. 80.
24 TF, pp. 128–30.
25 TF, p. 133.
26 TF, p. 235.
27 Interview in *Hibernia,* May 1964.
28 *Envoy,* vol. 3, no. 9, August 1950. C. Pr. p. 54.
29 C. Pr., pp. 35–6.

Chapter 3

1 Kavanagh quoted this stanza in the *RTV Guide,* 20 November 1964.
2 C. Pr., p. 37.
3 *Irish Weekly Independent,* 16 February 1929.
4 *Dundalk Democrat,* 16 February 1929.

5 GF, p. 254.
6 GF, p. 254.
7 K. H. Connell, 'Peasant Marriage in Ireland'. *Econ. Hist. Review*, vol. xiv, no. 3, 1962.
8 KW, no. 9, 7 June 1952, p. 4.
9 SP, p. 6.
10 *The Dublin Magazine*, January–March 1938.
11 C. Pr., p. 176.
12 *The Bell*, vol. xvii, no. 7, October 1951.
13 Private letter to the writer, 11 August 1964.
14 *Standard*, 12 June 1942.
15 *Lapped Furrows*, p. 57.
16 *Ibid.*, p. 58.

Chapter 4
1 W. B. Yeats, *Essays*. Macmillan, 1924. p. 492.
2 *Envoy*, no. 2, January 1950. p. 85.
3 *Irish Times*, 13 November 1943. Book review.
4 *Standard*, 5 October 1945.
5 *Envoy*, no. 12, November 1950. p. 77.
6 *New Statesman*, 5 February 1949.
7 Unused draft of a radio talk entitled 'The Inspired Idiot'. Much of the material in this talk was later broadcast under the title 'A Goat Tethered outside the Bailey', (Radio Eireann, 2 February 1953).
8 *The Bell*, Summer 1953. 'A Goat Tethered outside the Bailey'.
9 Draft radio talk. See 8 above.
10 IFJ, 15 November 1958.
11 IFJ, 8 August 1959.
12 IFJ, 11 August 1962.
13 IFJ, 25 July 1959.
14 KW, no. 11, 21 June 1952.
15 *Ibid.*
16 Guinness lecture at the Queen's University, Belfast, 27 November 1964.
17 IFJ, 16 May 1959.
18 C. Pr., p. 63.
19 'Thinking of Other Things.' BBC Third Programme, 20 February 1951.
20 TF, p. 233.
21 KW, no. 13.

Chapter 5
1 *Nimbus*, vol. 3, no. 3, summer 1956.
2 *Irish Times*, 28 February 1952.
3 *Ibid.*, 1 August 1942.
4 *Ibid.*, 3 October 1942.
5 *The Standard*, 31 May 1946.
6 *RTV Guide*, 13 December 1963.
7 *The Standard*, 3 January 1947.
8 *The Bell*, September 1951.

9   KW, no. 12.
10 *Envoy*, September 1950.
11 *Envoy*, June 1950.
12 IFJ, 15 November 1958.
13 KW, no. 9.
14 *Envoy*, July 1951.
15 *Ibid.*, July 1950.
16 *Ibid.*, December 1949.
17 *Irish Times*, 13 January 1945.
18 *Ibid.*, 13 January 1945.
19 BBC Third Programme, 30 July 1951.
20 IFJ, 30 June 1962.
21 *Envoy*, April 1951.
22 KW, no. 12.
23 *Ibid.*
24 *Ibid.*
25 *Ibid.*
26 KW, no. 3.
27 *Envoy*, January 1950.
28 *The Bell*, December 1947.
29 *Envoy*, January 1950.
30 *The Bell*, December 1947.
31 *The Standard*, 21 March 1947.
32 KW, no. 12.
33 *Ibid.*
34 *Hibernia*, July-August 1964.

Chapter 6
1   SP, p. 27.
2   C. Pr., pp. 174–5.
3   IFJ, 18 October 1958.
4   IFJ, 9 March 1963.
5   *Studies*, vol. xlviii, 1959, p. 29.
6   Poetry Book Society Bulletin, no. 25, June 1960.
7   *Studies*, vol. xlviii, 1959, p. 33–4.
8   SP, p. 25.

Chapter 7
1   *Irish Times*, 27/28 March 1964. Maurice Kennedy reviewing *Self-Portrait*.
2   *Two Rivers*, vol. 1, no. 1.
3   *The Chicago Review*, vol. 17, nos. 2/3, 1964.
4   *Threshold*, vol. 5, no. 1, Spring/Summer, 1961.
5   IFJ, 1 April 1961.
6   C. Pr., p. 93.
7   *Ibid.*
8   C. Pr., p. 98.
9   IFJ, 1 September 1962.

10 *Ibid.*
11 IFJ, 29 November 1958.
12 GF, p. 11.
13 *Envoy*, July 1951.
14 Boswell: Life of Johnson, Oxford University Press, 1953, vol. 1, p. 398.
15 Boswell: *op. cit.*, vol. II, p. 652.
16 *The Bell*, April 1948.
17 *Ibid.*
18 SP, p. 13.
19 Boswell: *op. cit.*, vol. 1, p. 323.
20 IFJ, 13 June 1955.
21 Boswell: *op. cit.*, vol. II, p. 496.
22 Boswell: *op. cit.*, vol. I, p. 263.
23 *Nimbus*, Summer 1956.
24 BBC Welsh Region, 22 March 1963.
25 *The Bell*, April 1948.
26 *Essays and Introductions*, Macmillan 1961, p. 522.
27 *The Standard*, 28 March 1947.
28 *Hail and Farewell*, Heinemann, Uniform edition, vol. 3, p. 103.
29 *Selected Essays*, Faber 1964.
30 *National Observer*, July 1959.
31 *November Haggard*, p. 68.
32 *Envoy*, July 1950.

Chapter 8
1 See Chapter 4, note 8.
2 *RTE Guide*, 7 October 1966.
3 *The Bell*, January 1954.
4 SP, p. 29.
5 *Studies*, Spring 1959.
6 *Hibernia*, May 1964.
7 *Irish Times*, 4 March 1944.

Chapter 9
1 Boswell: *Life of Johnson*, Oxford University Press, 1933, vol. ii, p. 244.
2 BBC Third Programme, 13 May 1960.
3 *The Backward Look*, p. 299. Macmillan, 1967.
4 GF, p. 143.
5 TF, p. 235.
6 TF, p. 63.
7 A Selection of Poems and Prose, ed. W. H. Gardner. Penguin, 1953, p. 122.
8 X, vol. 2, no. 2. August 1961.
9 'Shakespeare's Sonnets', *The Listener*, 9 July 1964.
10 *The Standard*, 5 October 1945.
11 Lady Gregory, *Journals 1916–1930*, ed. Lennox Robinson. Putnam, 1946, p. 262.
12 *November Haggard*, p. 73.

INDEX

140

141